WHEN THE THRUSH CALLS

WHEN THE THRUSH CALLS

Rachel O'Neal

Wordscape Publishing

ISBN: 0-9761707-0-1

Cover design and illustration by Lauren O'Neal
Page Layout by Anita Jones

Photo on back cover is Grizzly Peak in Ashland, Oregon

For Greg and Dan

Forever in my heart

This is a true story. The names have been changed to protect privacy. Some minor details may be altered.

"What we call the beginning is often the end
And to make an end is to make a beginning.
The end is where we start from." (T.S. Eliot)

1

On a warm August day in 1995, my sister, Rose, and I headed into the back country south of Mt. Rainier. We were in my Honda Civic with two fully loaded packs in the seat behind us. In the past, my mood would lighten with each mile that drew me closer to wilderness. But not on this day. Even after a night spent camping nearby, a heaviness I normally associated with my urban existence remained. Today the wilderness seemed like a strange mother offering to suckle an inconsolable, abandoned child who would never see her real mother again.

We drove into the trailhead parking lot and I guided our vehicle into a spot opposite our trail. We had traveled more than three hours the previous day, some of that time on rough roads. After camping at the nearby lake last night, we headed here this morning.

I had been here several times before. Goat Rocks Wilderness had been one of Garth's and my favorite spots. This was Rose's first visit.

We got out of the car and hauled the packs out to lean on the car while we laced up our hiking boots. There were only a couple other vehicles in the big dirt lot. I was glad we had been able to come mid-week; I wanted us to have as much solitude as possible. The air felt cool, though the sun was warm. I looked up at the sky, which for the moment was clear. "Looks like the weather plans to cooperate," I commented to Rose. "That's nice. Once when Garth and I hiked in here, we got snowed on during the night."

I felt Rose's bemused glance, "You told me about that."

"That was the time Goat Lake was frozen. We were camped at the lake and woke up to a couple inches of snow. Garth managed to fix us coffee at the entrance to our tent before we headed down. We huddled there, looking out on that magical snow world, sipping our hot brew. I remember seeing Clark's nutcrackers in the trees that morning."

Rose pointed north. "Look at those clouds over there, Annie. Do you think they're coming this way?"

I looked at the dark clouds, but the sky overhead was still blue. I shrugged. "Ready?" I asked.

We started down the trail. I usually loved the crunch of hiking boots on a path, but today nothing so far had lifted the heaviness in my chest. A sign announced our entrance into Goat Rocks Wilderness. I stopped and allowed Rose to catch up. "Here we go," I said. "Garth always wanted you to do this with us."

Rose's face was alight and her eyes danced as she took in our surroundings. I recognized her excitement, but I could not share in it.

Shortly after we passed the sign, something flitted around in a bush by the trail. I stopped to investigate. Soon I spotted the robin-like bird with a bluish back, dark necklace, and orange belly: A varied thrush. I became flushed with a sense of Garth's presence. I watched it a few moments as it stared out at me. When Rose reached me I tried to point it out, but it was gone. "It was a thrush," I said.

"Ah," she said.

The last time I hiked this trail, Garth was in the lead. I could practically see him in front of me, his pack blocking a clear view of his head. I could see the way his feet landed. It was as if we had been here yesterday. Tears sprung to my eyes. How could he not be here? Why was he not here? All the questions. All the pain. Mother wilderness' milk tasted like gall today.

Our path wound on through the thick woods and began a steady slow climb. I planned for us to climb the 2,000 feet into alpine country and almost to Goat Lake today. It was only six miles and not a terribly steep climb, but I was already beginning to feel the 30 pounds on my back.

By noon, when we stopped for lunch, I welcomed the chance to lean my pack's weight against a tree for awhile. Rose relinquished hers with relief as well. We sat on boulders next to the trail and munched our cheese, dried fruit, and crackers. Although we were deep in the woods, I could see that those north clouds were beginning to cover the blue in the sky. They looked ominous.

Rose followed my gaze upward. "Do you think it's going to rain?"

"You never know what's going to happen in the mountains."

"How much farther do we have to go?"

We spread out the trail map between us. I pointed to our possible camping spot, a little before Goat Lake in an alpine meadow. "I think we're about halfway."

After lunch we hauled our supply loaded packs onto our now complaining backs and headed on. I had imagined being in the wilderness would have its usual effect of bringing me to present time. But even here the heaviness would not lift, the confusion clear. All I could think about was Garth's absence. His pack was here, but Rose hauled it, not Garth. Where was he?

The afternoon wore on, as our hike became a trudge. The darkness of the sky deepened. I hoped the impending rain would wait until we set up camp and ate dinner. In spite of my mood, I could not ignore the beauty around us. As we ascended, the trees thinned out and wildflowers became plentiful.

It was late afternoon before we reached the meadow. A lone tree on one end provided cover for a good spot to pitch the tent. After we had done just that, I stood on what had become our verandah and pointed south to where we would see Mount Adams on a clear day. I had a photo of Garth standing on this very spot, looking at me, with Mount Adams looming behind him. Today the clouds shrouded Mount Adams' visage.

We cooked a prepackaged lightweight dinner. Pretty minimalist eating for Rose and I, who were both better than average cooks.

We could see Goat Lake to the north. It did not look frozen. I hoped to hike the mile there the next day. Only minutes after cleaning up, we felt the first sprinkles. It was not entirely dark yet, but we were both exhausted, so entered our tent and went to sleep.

I woke early to steady rain on our tent. A lightness beyond our nylon protection told me it was morning. Checking my watch, I saw it was nearly six a.m. I lay in my bag resisting the urge to go out into that wet. Rose was sleeping soundly. I wondered what our day would be like if it kept raining. The slight memory of a dream trickled into my consciousness. I couldn't quite recall it, but suddenly I was flooded with a memory of my father as he sang, "Pinkety Dinkety Dinkety Dink, Pinkety Dinkety Do, I love you. Pinkety Dinkety Dinkety Dink, Pinkety Dinkety Do, I love you. I love you in the morning and I love you late at night. I love you when you're with me and I love you out of sight. So, Pinkety Dinkety Dinkety Dink, Pinkety Dinkety Do, I love you!"

The memory startled me. I hadn't thought about that song forever. Never before in my adult life had I recalled that my father had sung it or when he had sung it. The urge to go out brought me back to the present and our dismal morning. It sounded like the steady patter on our tent was much less and I wondered if the rain had stopped. I decided to venture out. My stirrings caused some movement in the bag next to me, but Rose didn't open her eyes or speak.

I went out into the dreary day. The rain had stopped for the moment and the drippings on our tent came from the tree we were camped under. I went to a spot some distance away to do my business. Though it wasn't raining, the sky promised a continuation of the night's wetness. The thought depressed me. As I crouched down, I heard the distinct single note call of a varied thrush. I was flooded with thoughts of Garth and tears filled my eyes. Yet, as the thrush continued to call, I felt the beauty of hearing this tuneful bird's call on a rainy day in the wilderness. It lifted my sadness a little and I reentered our tent with a slight joy hovering around the edges of my despair.

Rose spoke sleepily from the mound on her side of the tent. "Is it still raining?"

As I crawled back into my bag I said, "It's stopped for the moment, but I don't think it's done yet."

She groaned.

"Do you remember that Pinkety Dinkety song Dad used to sing?"

Rose turned to me with her full attention. "What made you think of that?"

"I woke with that tune going through my head this morning. Do you remember him singing that to us?"

"Yeah, boy I haven't thought about that in years!"

"When did he used to sing it to us?"

Rose grimaced. "This is pretty intense thinking you're expecting first thing in the morning. You know I'm not used to early mornings."

"Sorry."

She thought a moment. "It must have been when we were little, before the beatings started," she stopped. Then, "Do you remember that picture of us as babies where I'm hugging Dad?"

"I don't know if I do."

"He's holding both of us and I'm hugging his neck. I've often thought about that picture. There must have been a time when things were all right, you know? I think he sang that song to us when we were quite small."

"I wonder what changed."

"Well, we both remember going to Mom in the kitchen to protect us."

"Yeah, we were maybe four? Perhaps that was the first beating."

"At four. That's when Gary was born. Do you suppose something happened between Dad and Mom around Gary being born?"

"You mentioned Mom told you once Gary was unexpected. The fourth kid could have been too much for Mom. Maybe something happened then to shift Mom's attitude toward Dad and his frustration began the violence."

"It certainly seems there was a time before the beatings. A time when we have good memories of Dad."

I began to sing the Pinkety Dinkety song and Rose joined me. It lightened our spirits enough that we could get up to brave the weather.

Showers continued throughout the morning and we dodged the rain while we fixed ourselves hot cereal and tea. We still could not see Mount Adams. But we continued to hear the single note call of varied thrushes throughout the dreary beginning of our day. Each time I heard the call, I felt great sadness tinged with joy slip into my heart. After we cleaned up and put everything away, we donned our rain gear, put lunch food and water in our daypacks, and headed to Goat Lake.

The hike to the lake seemed easy compared to yesterday's trudge, though we endured the occasional shower. The closer we got to the lake, the more I was overcome with disbelief. I could not believe that I was here at Goat Lake and Garth was not. We walked to the shore of the lake. There was no ice at all. I still remembered that time in the late 80's when Garth and I finally made it to the frozen lake over snow covered trails. We weren't sure where the snow stopped and the lake started.

"Let's go up to where Garth and I camped that time," I suggested.

We headed up to the top of a knoll. Garth and I camped here the time we got snowed on. But there was a second time when the weather had been beautiful, with mountain goats in our site one morning of that trip. And I could almost see the Calliope hummingbird we saw flitting around the knoll.

I felt the heaviness of being here without him.

"Rose," I said. "Can I have a few minutes alone here before we eat?"

Rose looked at me a moment. "Sure," she said, "I'll be down by the lake. Come find me when you're ready."

I nodded.

I waited until she was out of sight and earshot.

"Damn you, Garth!" I swore. The rage inside me felt torrential. "Why aren't you here! Why? I hate you for not being here!" I threw a rock off the knoll and heard it hit the ground somewhere below. "God damn you, Garth!" I could remember exactly where we pitched our tent that time we had the goats. I could even remember where we took our shits. "God damn you, Garth, for not being here!"

And then the tears came like a sudden falls. Why? It was a question I could not answer. I sat on a rock and stared out at the gorgeous landscape. The beauty refused to offer a salve for my wound.

After about 20 minutes, I decided to go find Rose. She was sitting by the lake's shore.

"Are you okay?" she asked.

"No," I said. She said nothing. As I stood next to Rose on the bank, I took my binoculars out of my pack and began to search the hill on the other side of the lake.

"There are goats around here," I said. "There may..." and then I spotted one, two, a small group. I handed the glasses to Rose, "Up there, Rose, mountain goats."

"Oh wow," she said, "Cool!"

We watched the goats for awhile and then took out our cheese and dried fruit. The rain had stopped, but it was still cloudy and the clouds had darkened.

It was too chilly to sit for long, so we hiked back toward our campsite. We were about halfway when a hawk swooped down into the ravine to our right. It landed a few feet from a rather large mammal. I peered through my binocs. Just as my oversized eyes focused on the scene, the mammal lunged at the hawk. The hawk flew off. I couldn't identify the mammal from this distance, but I recognized that behavior.

I handed Rose the binocs, "Down there, Rose, a wolverine!"

I went on, "The size seems right. Garth and I once saw a wolverine about a football field away. It looked at us and moved toward us in a threatening way before heading in a different direction. I've heard they're pretty mean."

Rose was studying the animal. "It's a pretty good size. Wow, a wolverine!"

"I'm glad it's not any closer."

"Do you think it would hurt us?"

"I don't know. But I do know it's not afraid of us."

Rose handed me the glasses so I could take another look. "Fantastic!" she said.

When we returned to camp, we made a small fire to ward off the damp. The occasional showers were light now. We sat by the fire before beginning our dinner preparations. I asked Rose about Arnie, her husband, and about her work as an emergency room nurse. But my mind was only half engaged. Part of me, a lot of my attention, was on an earlier time — a time several years ago before any of this had happened; or at least before we knew what was going on.

———

It was early October in 1992. Garth and I were vacationing at Malheur Wildlife Refuge in Eastern Oregon. We knew something was not totally right with Garth, but neither of us was giving it conscious attention. We were camped at Page Springs. We had had a lovely day birding in the Refuge and had just finished hiking over a mile up a stream near our site following the hoot of an owl, hoping to find and identify it. We had been unable to spot it, though we kept hearing it until its call seemed to drift away. We were peaceful after dinner as we sat around the campfire watching the flames.

"I love this place, sweetheart," I said.

"I know," said Garth.

When it was time to retire, Garth made his preparations and headed for the tent. He could never stand to disturb the fire, preferring to leave while it still burned strong. I waited until he was inside the tent and then separated the logs so the fire would go out.

During the night I woke to hooting owls. I lay in our bag listening. The hoots became a chorus, as owl after owl joined in until it seemed as if dozens of owls congregated in the trees around our tent singing in a grand owl chorale. Garth slept soundly and I was too stunned to wake him, not wanting to move and disturb the magical moment. The owls continued to serenade me for what seemed like an hour or more before, one by one, they dropped out until one lone hoot carried on. I lay in our tent in a state of bliss with the lone owl gently nudging me into a peaceful sleep.

I woke to Garth rummaging around outside. I joined him. He had started a fire and had water on the stove for coffee. He looked toward the campsite below us.

"They got a deer," was all he said, but I saw the deep frown on his face.

The carcass was strung up and someone was gutting the animal. There were several pickups parked at the site and many men bustling around. I turned away.

"I heard the shot this morning," he said. "I think they shot it in the refuge. I'm sure that's illegal."

Later in the day we would mention this to a ranger. We never learned if there were consequences imposed. We had planned to leave that day anyway and were glad to escape the hanging carcass. So we packed up after breakfast and the sobering scene of the morning prevented me from telling Garth about my midnight owl chorale.

———

As Rose and I cleaned up after dinner, the sky was beginning to clear. Before we headed into our tent for the night, we even saw stars. I had hope for a nice day tomorrow.

We woke to sun. Though a weight in my heart accompanied me everywhere these days, the sun cheered me a bit when we got up. I pointed out Mount Adams to the south.

"Too bad we have to hike out today, Rose. It looks to be a gorgeous day!"

The sun had brought out Rose's childlike excitement and she was exuberant as we prepared breakfast and ate. We took our time getting ready for the return hike, stopping often to gaze at the gorgeous view of Mount Adams. It was a beautiful, color-sprayed hike down into the forest below as an array of wildflowers surrounded us, and accompanied our steps, providing a satiating visual feast. I could not help but feel a soft strain of happiness playing gently in my still injured heart. For a few hours during our stupendous wildflower bedecked descent, beauty eased the pain that I had begun to believe would accompany me the rest of my days. When we reached our car, I felt a semblance of the peace I used to feel after wilderness trips of the past.

We leaned our packs against the car and sat down.

"Whew!" Rose said.

"I forgot to take Garth's walking stick, Rose. I had intended to leave it at Goat Lake."

She looked at me. She knew by this time how important ritual had become to my grieving process. I could see the slight panic in her eyes as she contemplated what my need for completion would require of us.

I smiled ruefully. "I think I'll lean it against the sign that marks the entry into Goat Rocks Wilderness, " I said.

"Good idea," was all she commented.

She waited, collapsed by the car, while I got Garth's stick and headed back up the trail. I placed the stick against the sign and stood back. "Goodbye to hiking in the wilderness with you ever again, sweetheart." I stood there looking at his stick while tears rolled down my face. How long would the tears continue to come? How long before I could go on? How long are you gone, sweetheart? How long?

2

In late February 1993, the phone rang at Garth's and my apartment. I went into the second bedroom to answer it. It was the doctor. I had been expecting his call, but I had not been expecting his information.

Without prelude he said, much as one would rip off a bandaid, knowing there was no way to avoid pain, "I'm sorry to tell you we found cancer."

I felt stunned, as one feels in dreams sometimes when the incongruous occurs. There is a disbelief, a knowing, that this cannot be real. But it was. I must have managed to say something because the doctor went on.

He wanted to see Garth right away to talk about treatment, today if possible. He said something about surgery and cure that I imagine was trying to instill hope, but his words seemed to be far away in some kind of tin can.

There was a silence and I realized I was expected to say something. "Hello?" he queried gently.

"I'm here," I said. "You want to see Garth today?"

"If possible."

"He's at work. I'll go tell him and see if we can get to your office right away. Say, an hour or so?"

"That'll be fine," the doctor said.

I hung up the phone and felt a new kind of invasive terror I had never experienced. I warded it off with action, heading down to my car. In a daze, focusing on my driving with quiet desperation, I drove to the natural food store where we both worked. I felt I was driving out of the world of the known into a cold, terrifying, unknown world. I tried to remain calm as I mounted the stairs inside the store to Garth's office and walked toward him, not wanting to betray in my face a knowledge that threatened to shatter our world together.

His back was to me and he was on the phone.

"We've almost got the whole ad sold," he was saying. "I'll probably finish this up tomorrow." He finished his phone call and hung up.

I went to him and put my hands on his shoulders.

He looked up at me. "Hey," he said. "What are you doing here?"

"The doctor called," I said as calmly as I could. "Come outside a moment."

He didn't seem to read the news in my face. "Okay," he said.

We went out into the parking lot.

"So what did he say, Annie?"

I decided to say it quickly, the way the doctor had. It seemed the best way. "They found cancer, sweetheart."

And I wished anything in the world could have prevented me from having said those words as I saw Garth's face furrow into a deep frown. "Damn," he said.

"He wants to see you."

"Now?"

"To discuss options."

The doctor thought they could get the tumor with surgery. He wanted us to see a surgeon and oncologist without delay. He expressed optimism saying that Garth would be okay.

That night I lay in bed unable to sleep. Garth had managed to drift off. I felt we had gotten off on a wrong path somewhere. How had this happened? Where was it leading?

——

Before meeting Garth, I hated winter, as I felt barricaded from the natural world. Though I attempted cross-country skiing in the past, I always spent most my time in the snow rather than gliding across it. Garth convinced me to try again, and took me to places that were level where I could learn to stay upright. I began to see that cross-country skiing could transform winter for me. On these skinny boards I could venture out into that natural world at a time of year that it normally felt foreboding.

As I became more confident, every chance we got we began to head to the nearby hills above Ashland, where we lived in those early years. Garth especially loved to be the first ones on a trail after a fresh snow, even though that meant "breaking trail," which was a lot of work. He relished this job and always volunteered to be the leader. Though he was usually the smallest person in any group we were part of, he broke trail for the rest of us.

Most winters we would travel to Bend for a cross-country ski trip. One winter in the mid 80's, we spent an entire week skiing in Bend. We pushed ourselves to ski every day. Our goal was to ski to the base of Broken Top on our final day, about a 12-mile round trip.

We woke that last morning to clouds. Garth called the snow report and told me, "Four to six inches of fresh snow, Annie!" Instead of being a stopper, knowing we would most likely need to break trail, this information was for Garth, a green light. I felt hesitant, but willing.

At a local restaurant we downed several cups of coffee with our breakfast. We loaded cheese and crackers, nuts, and chocolate into our packs. Garth had applied Maxiglide to our skis the night before so we would glide even if the snow was sticky.

We headed up to Dutchman Flat, where we planned to start our trek to Broken Top. Garth was disappointed to find that some early risers had beat us to the trail, but I was relieved that we wouldn't need to break trail the whole way. I figured at some point we'd be the only ones skiing all the way and would have our opportunity to create our path.

The day was crisp and cold. It wasn't snowing, but the clouds promised more soon. After attaching our skis to our boots and donning hats and gloves, we headed across the Flats before veering off into the woods. The trees were heavy with snow. As we passed, occasionally a branch would dump a load of the white stuff with a loud "whomp!" onto the snowy forest floor. We started up the trail that would gradually climb to Big Meadow. Though someone had preceded us, we didn't run into anyone on the trail.

By noon we reached Big Meadow and stopped for a bite to eat. Garth studied our trail map and showed it to me.

"Looks like we need to follow that road to Crater Ditch and then on up to the base of Broken Top."

"Do you think it's going to snow?" I looked at the ominous sky.

"I hope so!" said Garth.

"We better get going, Garth, if it's going to snow."

He smiled. "Okay, Annie."

It didn't start snowing until we reached the flats of Crater Ditch, just below Broken Top. Garth stopped to allow me to catch up to him.

He pointed ahead to the mountain. There was no skied track where he pointed. "Let's ski up toward Broken Top a ways, Annie. We can follow our own tracks back."

"If the snow doesn't cover them," I said.

Garth looked at me. "We'll make sure we head back before that happens."

I wanted to go ahead too, even though the falling snow made me feel cautious. "Okay, Garth. We better keep going."

He skied ahead of me, creating our track in the fresh snow. Though I was tired from our week of skiing and the day's climb, I couldn't help but feel exhilarated as we pushed toward the base of Broken Top with snow falling softly all around. All I could hear was the soft swish of our skis. Garth left an even track for me. I followed him across the smooth snowy surface.

All around us was snow: on the ground, draping the trees, and falling from the sky. We were the only ones in this winter wonderland of white leaving our small track to the base of Broken Top. Once, when I stopped to look back, I could see our single track leading all the way back to the Flats. When Garth almost reached Broken Top's base, he stopped and turned back to me. It was starting to snow hard.

When I reached him, he was smiling. "Isn't this great, Annie?" he said excitedly. Snow had transformed his brown beard and moustache to icy whiteness.

We both looked at the mountain before us, then back at our track. "I guess we better head back," said Garth, "before our track fills up."

Strangely, I felt resistant to his suggestion, though I knew it was right. Here we had nothing in our heads but snow. Snow had gotten into our brains. Everything inside and out was pure. "It's so beautiful, Garth," I said.

Garth looked all around before he said, "I know." He turned his skis around and headed back.

It was a rainy March day in 1993 that found Garth and I sitting in the oncologist's waiting room. Garth had taken a Xanax, an anti-anxiety medication that he had started using for these stressful doctor appointments. I could see the doctor examining x-rays in his office. He glanced out toward us almost guiltily, as if we had caught him doing something he shouldn't. He turned back to the films and I had a premonition that something was terribly wrong.

The doctor escorted us into his office and closed the door. He seemed to hesitate and began haltingly to tell us that there were suspicious shadows in the x-rays of Garth's liver and lungs. Garth seemed not to understand at first.

"What are you trying to tell us?" I asked.

And then he did it like the bandaid, ripping the lid off our world with the words, "It looks like the cancer has metastasized to your lungs and liver already." He pointed to some slightly dark splotches on the x-ray. "There's no point in doing the surgery. We should probably just consider chemo and radiation."

I had never heard the word metastatic before and it took awhile for it to sink in that this man was telling us Garth was going to die. I sat in shock and horror. I felt disbelief that these splotches on an x-ray could give a death sentence.

Garth responded with a kind of visceral anger I had rarely seen from him. He stood up and began pacing the doctor's office and demanded, "I am sick and tired of hearing nothing but doom and gloom since this whole thing began. It just keeps getting worse. First I have cancer. Then you're going to cut out part of me. Now you're telling me I'm going to die!" Garth confronted the doctor with an intensity that left me in awe. "I want you to find something positive to tell me right now. I want to hear something positive from you about this situation right now!"

The doctor stepped back from Garth and nervously glanced at the x-rays, "Well," he said, "the shadows are small, not very developed." He kept stumbling around trying to find something positive in the situation and I couldn't help being amused. I loved Garth for being angry. I loved him for making that doctor stumble around trying to find something positive to tell us.

Later, on the way home, I fell apart and blamed myself for the situation. "I should have made you go to the doctor last summer, sweetheart," I said. "I should have forced you to go when you had that bleeding."

Garth looked at me and then away. "At least they've stopped talking about cutting away part of me," he said.

That made me feel better.

I knew we were both crazy. But in that moment we found comfort in the relief we felt that Garth did not have to undergo surgery. At least that threat was gone.

3

In May, after Garth had undergone chemo and radiation, his brother Raul paid for us to go to Mexico and stay at his one-bedroom condo in Zihuatenejo. Raul met us there to show us around and then left us to enjoy 14 days of recuperation while he returned to his home in Tequisquiapan. It was strange to have such a beautiful backdrop for our life together, when it had taken a disturbing turn. Garth and I would ride Raul's scooter into Zihuatenejo for groceries or to have lunch. We also walked the cobbled streets. Garth often commented that we were practically the only "Gringos" around. He liked that, being immersed in another culture, another world.

One afternoon we had lunch at an outside restaurant where we ordered fish tacos and followed that with coconut ice cream covered with kahlua. Afterward we walked along the water and stopped to watch a young couple snuggling close on a bench facing the sea. Then Garth pointed out a tangle of wires on a pole above us. So disorderly it was. Probably an illegal arrangement in America. I took pictures of the amorous couple, the tangled wires, and of Garth looking at me with that familiar smile and the sea behind.

Raul's condo was close to a spectacular beach. The water was warm and Garth could not get over the fact that he could walk out quite far without becoming completely immersed. We sat under palupas on the beach and ordered guacamole and chips with cold beer from the nearby hotel. We read books.

We met a couple from the states those first few days, who seemed attracted to us. I knew people always liked Garth, but I wondered if there wasn't a kind of voyeurism in their interest once we had told them about Garth's cancer. We didn't speak about it at length, but I often thought I caught them looking at us with wonder. Like here are two people that are facing death. How do people do that? What is it like?

But Garth and I were not facing death. We were living life with this new unknown companion. It was like a presence that we were reminded of every time I mixed up the shark cartilage Garth was drinking as an alternative treatment. We were reminded of it when we walked to town one day and Garth's legs were hurting. He had been complaining of pain in his legs for months that the doctors had no explanation for. There was no longer just two of us. There was me, Annie. There was Garth. And there was cancer.

But we were not facing death. We were living with something we did not understand that frightened us.

One day on a walk near our abode, Garth and I spotted a cardinal that didn't look quite like a cardinal and then saw a flash of metallic blue in a bush. Though we were not in a particularly great spot for birding, I was thrilled with the local birds. I had never seen frigatebirds, which soared over the ocean like some kind of strange tropical hawk; great-tailed grackles, which were as common as crows in Zihuatenejo; or the stunning yellow-winged caciques. We managed to capture the blue bird with our binoculars well enough to identify it later as an orange-breasted bunting. The cardinal was Mexico's version.

One morning I woke early and while Garth still slept; I slipped out to the poolside in front of our place. I was seeking a hummingbird I'd seen flitting around. First, though, I spotted an unusual looking bird with an incredible large bill that I would later learn was a smooth-billed ani. My early rising was also rewarded with two hummingbirds I had never seen before: a cinnamon hummingbird and a spectacular violet sabrewing. I sat in a chair excited by the sighting of fantastic new birds. Yet beneath this love for the world that these choice bird sightings lifted me to, coursed a new scary threatening stream of fear. This chilling stream was beginning to feel unstoppable, almost inevitable.

I wondered, sitting beside a pool in Zihuatenejo, how one could hold great beauty and love in the same heart if there was also great sorrow.

———

It was during an extended trip in 1987 that Garth and I discovered Cape Lookout along the northern Oregon Coast. We were staying at the campground and had been dodging raindrops since our arrival. When we got up the second morning to clear skies, we decided to hike the trail out to the end of the Cape. We drove to the trailhead. There were several other cars in the parking lot.

At the beginning of the trail we studied the map. The map indicated a spot along the trail where a plaque commemorated the crash of a B-17 bomber in 1943. "Maybe we can find some remnants from the crash," suggested Garth. He headed down the trail that led deep into the coastal rainforest. I followed.

As we walked the trail, I welcomed the warm sun that shone on us after several days of intermittent showers. We had managed to stay dry, but Garth talked of finding a motel. I didn't want to do that, preferring to be outdoors, even though we weren't properly prepared for rain. Our tent had a rain fly that protected us at night, but we didn't have any rain tarps for our campsite. We had resorted to cooking off the end of our truck several times in the last few days, with the truck's canopy as minimal protection.

As the forest of sitka spruce and cedars deepened, my mind began to quiet. Though we had been on the road for several weeks now, the troubled waters of my mind were still murky. However, here in this forest that felt almost primeval, my mind began to clear. I felt myself entering the world of the forest and becoming more present. We got to the plaque about the bomber's crash.

Garth took off his pack and foraged off the trail looking for crash remnants. I waited for him, thinking about the lone survivor of this crash, wondering what that would have been like. Garth returned empty-handed.

"I don't suppose there'd be anything left after all this time," he admitted.

We started back up the trail toward the end of the Cape. We were almost to the end when we decided to stop for lunch at a point where we could sit overlooking a cove. Garth pulled our lunch out of his pack.

"Do you have the click yet, Garth?" I asked.

"Not quite," he said. "Do you?"

"For the first time this trip, I've finally got it." The "click" is from Tennessee Williams' "Cat on a Hot Tin Roof." It's the way a character in the play, Brick, described the feeling he got from drinking. He would drink until he got the "click" and nothing bothered him anymore. Garth and I used that term to describe the calm and ease that we would usually feel after a few days away from our normal routine. This "click" resulted in a clear, unperturbed mind.

We were eating our lunch near the end of the Cape when Garth pointed and said excitedly, "Look over there, Annie. Whales!"

I saw two big dark shapes cavorting in the ocean. Garth pulled out our binoculars. "There's a little school of them!" he proclaimed.

He handed me the binoculars. I saw several large dark bodies diving and surfacing. We kept trading the binoculars until the whales moved further off shore and out of sight.

"Wow!" said Garth. "Now I've got the click!"

After lunch, we headed to the end of the Cape. Everything seemed bright, fresh and crisp in this clear present state of mind. We greeted another couple having their lunch on the rocks right where the Cape's final finger of land jutted out into the ocean. The whales were nowhere in sight.

The sun favored us the rest of the day with its presence in the sky. As we made our dinner preparations at the picnic table under the welcome clear sky, I heard a loud hammering. In the old snag nearby, I saw a large bird that seemed responsible. I trained our binoculars on the bird and brought a huge woodpecker with a large red crest into focus. I handed the binoculars to Garth.

"Look at that!" I instructed.

While Garth studied the bird, I flipped through our bird book to the woodpeckers and found the only one it could be, a pileated. I showed it to Garth. He handed me the binocs and looked at the book.

"A pileated, Annie, that's a PID for us!" Garth and I had begun to identify birds on this trip and when we became convinced that we had a positive identification on a bird that we had seen for the first time, we awarded it with PID.

The loud hammering reverberated throughout the campground as we watched our first pileated woodpecker search for its dinner. I felt great excitement at seeing a new bird and identifying it for the first time. It seemed so amazing to me that our world had contained these beautiful creatures and I had never seen them or at least never paid attention before.

As I continued to watch the woodpecker, Garth made a record in our bird book of this first sighting. We were beginning to collect quite a few PIDs that Garth faithfully marked in our book. When our now familiar feathered friend finally flew off, we settled down to enjoy our dinner.

4

In summer 1993, Garth and I moved from our apartment into a rented house in the hills of northwest Portland. Garth had wanted to buy a house when we first moved to Portland six years previously, but I had resisted. Having just sold a problem house before moving to Portland, that my first husband Dave and I had owned; I wasn't ready to enter that realm again. Renting a house was a compromise. I was worried enough about Garth's illness at this point that I was beginning to do whatever he wanted.

The house was the farthest back of three on a large piece of property. It had a deck out back with a view of the meadow behind that had a few cedars growing around the edges. We felt we had moved out of the city, even though we could be in town in about 20 minutes. We heard hooting owls and yelping coyotes at night. Garth even saw a coyote at the edge of the meadow early one morning.

I put up bird feeders and Garth talked about starting a garden. We had a few barbecues on the deck with friends.

We could almost believe we had a life again, except for the darkness crouching in a corner of our minds, ready to spring out at any moment. We had different attitudes toward this threat. Garth kept expecting the doctors to save him. I don't think he ever embraced that they viewed him as incurable, stage 4, terminal. Though I was no more accepting of a terminal prognosis, I understood the doctors' perspective, that their radiation and chemo were only stop gaps to hopefully prolong Garth's now short life. I felt we had to reach beyond mainstream medicine to something alternative if he was to survive. I began researching what that alternative might be.

It was a frustrating journey. I studied alternatives I found out about in the library and called various programs to get more information. My writing background served me well in this task that began to seem daunting. How to sift the wheat from the chaff? There seemed to be numerous options available that offered hope, yet all our insurance would pay for were radiation and chemo, neither of which would do more than delay what his doctors seemed to view as inevitable.

We were already doing the shark cartilage, but both of us were becoming disillusioned with this process. I would mix up the cartilage for Garth in a glass of juice. Still, the smell was so nauseating, Garth had to hold his nose to drink the stuff and follow it with a shot of breath freshener afterward to destroy the disgusting aftertaste. His throat always felt scratchy and he was beginning to lose his appetite.

I remember the moment we realized we could not do the shark cartilage anymore. We were at the coast with some old high school friends of Garth's. One of them had fixed a chicken dinner for Garth, a favorite. We sat in front of plates heaped with chicken, potatoes, corn and salad.

I looked at Garth across the table. He was staring at his plate of food with the most heartbreaking mixture of desire and repulsion. Our eyes met in shared disappointment and fear.

Later that night in our bedroom at the house on the coast, I broached the subject. "Sweetheart," I said tentatively, "Maybe we should stop the cartilage."

I was standing next to the bed that Garth was sitting on. He had already lost ten pounds since our ordeal had begun and as he was such a small person to begin with, this left him with no reserve. He finished taking off his shoe and then looked at me. "I was thinking the same thing."

"You've got to be able to eat."

"Yes."

And so we stopped it. Though this choice frightened me, as now our only hedge against this potent foe was more chemo, I also felt relief. Garth began eating a little more.

I stepped up my search among the alternative treatments available, rejecting anything that was prohibitively expensive; that wasn't particularly effective against Garth's type of cancer; or about which I got weird vibes when talking with the method's proponents on the phone. I narrowed our options down to one, 714X, a treatment developed by Gaston Naessens, a French scientist living and working in Canada.

Naessens saw cancer as a problem with the immune system and decided it needed to be treated systemically, instead of bombarding it like it was an invasion. Naessens' 714X was composed of camphor molecules, nitrogen molecules, and organic salts. It was supposed to work by distracting the cancer cells with the camphor molecules, which cancer cells are attracted to, and feeding them with the nitrogen molecules so the cancer stops robbing the body of nitrogen. This reduced the stress to the immune system, thus allowing it to recover and start fighting the cancer on its own. The organic salts restored the lymph system; that had become sluggish and clogged with the cancer, to its normal liquid state, allowing the cancer cells to be flushed from the body.

Garth was somewhat skeptical, but would consider this. His brother, Raul, was willing to pay for it. Now, all I had to do was get a doctor to write a prescription for it and find somebody to teach me to administer it, as it required an unusual injection process. Meanwhile, we were uncomfortable with waiting for this all to fall into place before we did anything, so we agreed to another round of chemo.

I took Garth to the doctor's office and watched while they hooked him up to the dripping poison. He would read, or we would play cards, or sometimes I would leave and he would talk with the other patients. We both tried to make this okay. I think Garth still believed the chemo might save him.

———

In the spring of 1987, I sold the house that Dave and I had owned together in Ashland. Garth and I had been living in it for about three years. Garth had been working as a manager at the local natural foods co-op. I had been freelance writing and doing odd jobs. We decided we needed to move somewhere else to try and discover what we wanted to do with the rest of our lives. We had a huge garage sale, threw everything else into storage, and loaded our camping equipment into our '78 Toyota pickup.

Garth felt uncomfortable giving up our home. He always felt the need for his life to revolve around some home base. I gave him a card that said "Home is where the heart is" that we taped in our pickup's cab. It made him feel slightly better.

We headed out to discover our new home and to explore the great northwest. We planned to allow ourselves about six months to do this. We intended to mostly camp along the way.

We went down to California for a few days first to visit Rose, Dave, and Clare (Dave's wife). Then we headed over to the northern California coast. One of the first great spots we discovered on this trip was along the "lost coast." It is called that because when Hwy. 1 was built, this part of the coast was too rugged to build a major road. So the builders were forced inland. A portion of this part of the coast was declared a wilderness area and saved from development.

After a night at a place called Usal Camp, we turned north again. Garth had discovered a squiggly thing called Usal Road on our map. He marked this as our route. When we got to it, I hesitated. This "road" was a rutted dirt widening in the forest.

"Garth," I complained, "I'm not sure this is such a great idea."

Garth always wanted to take the roads less traveled. I could not deny him when he gave me that look: a combination of pleading and excitement.

So he turned our pickup we had named "Truckie" onto this "road." Truckie bounced and careened through the ruts and dips. I began questioning my wisdom in giving Garth his head with this. After a half-hour or so of probably five mile an hour travel at best, I asked wistfully, "I don't suppose we could turn back?"

I didn't really expect him to respond because there was no way to turn around. His lips were pursed with concentration as he navigated Truckie through the next vehicle-swallowing mud hole.

"Do you suppose we could get stuck out here?" I asked nervously.

Again, Garth didn't respond and I realized he was trying to make sure Truckie didn't stop in case we couldn't get her going again. His lack of response quelled my conversation as I realized Garth was nervous. And that made me tense up. I gripped the door handle on my side as we jerked and jolted through the next few ruts.

Silence reigned for the next hour. I noticed Garth's grip on the steering wheel was making his knuckles turn white.

"How much further do you think we have to go?" I asked.

Garth glanced at me and then turned quickly back to his careful navigating. "Don't know," he ventured.

"Jesus, Garth!"

He knew better than to respond to that and we drove on in silence for another hour or more before the road began to level out and become drivable. It took awhile for the tension in Truckie's cab to lessen. When we finally arrived at the end of Usal Road and confronted an intersection, a hitchhiker flagged us down.

He came up to Garth's window. He was bearded, long haired, and about 25. I didn't want anything to do with him or anything else at that moment.

"You guys headed down to Sinkyone?" he asked.

"What's that?" asked Garth. I wished he would just say no and head out of there. There wasn't a car in sight and nothing but dirt roads in every direction. I felt suspicious and fearful of this man who had appeared out of nowhere.

The guy pointed to the dirt road to our left that veered down. "It's a wilderness area right on the coast down that road about two miles. It's fantastic. You really ought to check it out, and I could use a ride down there. I've got my pack in the bushes over there."

I couldn't believe Garth was talking to this stranger. Who was this man and what the hell was he doing?

"Sounds cool," said Garth calmly as if we hadn't just been miraculously saved from being stranded in the mud somewhere back on Usal Road. "What do you think, Annie?"

"No," I quipped, "I've had enough of dirt roads!"

Garth looked disappointed and the guy outside his window looked like he couldn't believe his luck that the one car that happened along wasn't going to give him a ride. "Oh man," he said. "You guys really ought to go down there!"

"No," I said firmly to Garth.

The guy shrugged and went off toward the bushes.

Garth looked at me. "Come on Annie, it's only two miles and he said it's the greatest! It won't be like Usal. That must have been 25 or 30 miles!"

I looked away from him. "Let's eat some lunch and then decide what we're going to do."

We sat on the back of the truck eating sandwiches. Garth studied the map. He showed me Sinkyone. "It looks pretty cool, Annie. And the road isn't nearly as squiggly as Usal."

I was beginning to relent. Garth so wanted to do it and the part of me that believed in guidance was having trouble finding our lone hitchhiker turning up out of nowhere to be a mere happenstance. Was he directing us to Sinkyone? Had he been sent at that particular time?

Garth sensed my weakening and began to talk excitedly about camping on the coast. By the time we were done with lunch, he had won again.

We turned Truckie down Sinkyone's dirt road and entered another world. Some things seem handed to us from God. As we descended into Sinkyone Wilderness, my mind cleared of worries and concerns. I felt myself moving into present time. The road seemed exciting instead of treacherous; the fog shrouded trees gorgeous. When we reached the bottom we left the fog for brilliant sun.

In front of us was a dazzling, pristine, foaming coastline that was met by rocky black sand. Our eyes met and said without a word, wow. We stayed at Sinkyone for three days that visit. We were to come back to this special place several more times. I believe Sinkyone may have been Garth's favorite spot on the planet. It was on this first visit that I took one of my best pictures of him. He is sitting nude on a rock at Bear's Harbor looking out at the ocean. I called to him just before I snapped his picture. So in the foreground of this shot, Garth's naked body is turned sideways with him looking back at me with that bemused smile, while the rocky black beach heads out to the deep blue ocean beyond.

5

By December, ten months into our ordeal, Garth had gone through two regimens of chemo, yet the cancer continued to advance. He was down from 125 pounds to about 100 pounds. I was holding out for some kind of miracle from the 714X. I'm not sure Garth had much hope in this alternative treatment, but he didn't know what else to do. His doctors offered nothing and held out no hope. His chemo doctor had written the prescription for us for the 714X and said he would help us learn the unusual injection process. Rose, who was a nurse, had agreed to come to Portland and help us learn the process as well. Naessens' company had sent me several videos describing this process that I gave to Rose and Garth's doctor.

Rose arrived a few days before Christmas. We planned to start the 714X right after the holiday. When I approached the doctor about setting up an appointment to discuss the injection process, I discovered he had not even looked at the video. Rose reassured me we could do this without the doctor's help if necessary. We did meet with the doctor so Rose could ask him some questions she had concerning the process.

The injection procedure was complicated. Because 714X turns into a gas when it meets body temperature, the area where it's going to be injected has to be cooled so as not to cause pain. This was accomplished by placing ice packs on the groin area at the injection site for five to ten minutes. Then the injection site must be discovered by first locating the femoral artery so that it wasn't hit inadvertently with the needle.

Once the site was found, the injection had to be done slowly over 15 to 20 minutes. After the injection was complete, another ice pack had to be applied to the area for 15 to 20 minutes to slow down the entrance of the gas into the lymph.

The tension in our living room that first night was evident. Garth lay down on the couch. I felt uncertain, wondering how I would learn to give Garth these injections. Garth's face was drawn and white. He seemed to be gritting his teeth.

Rose was bustling between the kitchen and the couch with her professional nursing demeanor. She placed the ice pack.

"I'm putting it right here, Annie. See?"

I tried to focus through my anxiety.

"My legs hurt," Garth said.

"Try moving them a little, Garth," suggested Rose.

Garth moved restlessly. "It's hard for me to keep them straight out like this," he said.

Inwardly, I was wringing my hands, but I tried to convey a calm exterior.

At the appointed time, Rose drew up the proper amount of 714X into a syringe. She removed the ice pack and felt for the femoral artery. When she found it she had me feel it too so I would know what I was looking for.

Garth's eyes were wide with terror.

Without hesitating, Rose plunged the needle in and began the slow injection process. Garth winced.

"It's okay, Garth," she said. "Everything seems to be going fine. Try to relax and breathe."

Garth's body seemed rigid.

Finally it was time for the ice pack again. Rose placed it and headed back into the kitchen to put things away. I followed her.

"How am I going to do this, Rose, with Garth feeling so anxious?"

"Don't worry, Annie, you'll do fine."

"But do you think the treatment can work if he's terrified of it?"

"Yes," she said.

I didn't know if she believed this herself, but she knew what she had to say. If I was going to do this, I had to have some confidence. This first night the whole thing seemed impossible.

But the next night, Rose insisted I do the whole procedure myself, with her there simply to guide and coach.

Now, both Garth and I were terrified. Garth's look as I filled up the syringe would have been enough to make me go screaming out of the room if Rose's calm nursing presence hadn't kept edging the situation toward completion.

"That's right, Annie," she said with placidity. She checked to make sure I had found the femoral artery. When I looked at her after pinpointing the injection site, she nodded. "Go ahead," she reassured me, "you're not going to hurt him."

I plunged the needle in and felt Garth jerk. I glanced at him and saw his look of terror.

"It's okay, Garth," said Rose. "She's found the right spot."

I was so relieved when we were done. I did not know how I was going to do this every night for 21 days.

But I did. After Rose left, I stuck him every night and he endured it. We were allowed a 3-5 day break before the next 21-day series.

Garth and I headed over to the coast for a couple nights. We tried to cheer ourselves with an espresso at a coffee shop on the way over. It helped slightly, but Garth's inability to eat more than about one quarter of a bagel terrified me. I was beginning to feel a panic inside me. What would we do if the 714X failed us? What next? How could he survive if he couldn't eat anything?

At the coast, Garth collapsed on the couch facing our window with an ocean view. I didn't even ask him if he wanted to walk on the beach. His legs were so painful at this point, that any unnecessary walking simply was not done.

I set him up with fluids and a blanket.

"Do you need anything else, sweetheart?"

"I'm fine, Annie. Why don't you go for a walk on the beach?"

"I was thinking I might do that. Are you sure you'll be okay?"

"Go," he said.

I went outside and down the steps of our motel complex that lead to the beach. It was a cloudy day, but not wet. I breathed the salty air as I strolled closer to the water. The ocean roar slammed into my awareness. Here it seemed things went on as they always had. One wave following another. Constantly. Never ending.

I glanced up toward our motel and thought I could see Garth's body in the window of our room. This was the first time we had been to the coast together and I was on the beach alone. It felt strange, unreal. Part of me did not understand why he was not with me.

Another part of me felt calmed by the water rushing toward me. I walked along its edge just avoiding contact. The calmness rushed over me for a few moments until it receded and was replaced by a panic that tugged at me like a ruthless undertow. I could not seem to control either phenomenon, but was pulled back and forth between peace and panic like they were currents inside me arising and falling of their own accord.

Garth was not physically with me, but I felt his presence like a cloak. Every thought was imbedded with Garthness. When I returned to the room, I did not feel that we had been apart.

———

One summer in the late 80's, as Garth and I walked through the deep old growth forest of Bull of the Woods, on our way to camp at Big Slide Lake, he stopped and brought my attention to a haunting single note bird's call.

"Listen," he whispered, as if we were in some cathedral and he didn't want to disturb anyone.

I heard the tuneful note emitting from somewhere above us. It sounded like someone was playing a single note on a flute. "What is it?" I asked.

"I don't know," Garth whispered again. He often would whisper when we were in the woods, and I got into the habit of whispering back. Once I asked him mid-whisper, "Why are we whispering?" He responded as if it should be obvious, "We shouldn't disturb them, it's their home." I knew better than to ask him who "them" was. "Them" was whoever or whatever lived here, the plants and animals. Garth loved going into the woods, but he had an understanding about us being visitors in someone else's home.

The single note call continued. "I think it must be a bird," said Garth. "I love that call."

We heard the call on many backpack trips and hikes for the next couple years before we discovered what it was for sure. Garth often stopped to listen to it and it became a favorite forest sound for us both.

As we became more serious about bird identification and bird calls, we acquired binoculars and a bird guidebook. Then one birthday, Garth gave me a tape of recorded bird calls. I was listening to it one afternoon in our apartment, while Garth and some friends worked on some computer project in the study.

Suddenly I heard the single note call we had noticed so often in the woods. I was so stunned and excited, I missed the verbal notation of the bird's name. I rewound the tape quickly and replayed the call. Some knowledgeable birder's voice supplied the answer to our mystery, "varied thrush." I knew what varied thrushes looked like, remembered seeing them on the coast at a favorite spot near Yachats, but had never associated them with the call that had charmed many a wilderness trip. I called to Garth excitedly.

"Come here, Garth!"

"We're in the middle of something, Annie."

I went to the study door and three expectant, slightly irritated faces peered at me from the computer.

"Garth, you have to come hear this."

He got up from his chair reluctantly, knowing from my tone that he had no choice. Our friends stayed in the study looking at the computer screen.

Garth followed me to the living room of our apartment.

"What?" he asked.

I rewound the tape and played it again, "Listen," I said.

The single note call of a varied thrush filled our living room.

"Play it again," Garth said.

After hearing it a second time and its attribution, Garth looked at me, "Wow," he said.

"It's a varied thrush, Garth. Our call is a varied thrush!"

Garth smiled at me with amusement and understanding, "So it is, Annie, so it is."

6

After the third series of 714X, Garth and I were both discouraged. There was no evidence it was helping and his leg pain was becoming unbearable. Garth's doctor decided to do another bone scan to try and determine what was going on in Garth's legs.

We were not prepared for the results of this test. The doctor told us that it showed a fracture in Garth's right hip. I couldn't believe this, but now when I looked at Garth I could see it from the way his leg hung. I felt the doctor should have seen this long before. No wonder he had had so much pain trying to keep that leg still during the injections!

So now we had to face surgery, which was a frightening prospect. Garth only weighed about 80 pounds now. I asked the doctor if he thought Garth could tolerate the surgery. He said yes. This was the same doctor, of course, who had not detected the broken hip and who had told us at one point that we didn't have to worry about fractures.

But we had no choice. He had the surgery for a partial hip replacement on March 24. I was sitting in the waiting room with a couple friends when the surgeon finally came in and headed toward us. I steeled myself for the worst. When he said, "He came through fine," I felt unbelieving relief. I realized that I had been preparing myself for the doctor to tell me Garth wasn't going to make it.

"Can I see him?"

"He should be up in his room in a few minutes."

My friends and I headed to Garth's room and arrived just as he was being wheeled down the hall. We followed them into Garth's room. I went to his side and took his hand.

"Hi sweetheart," I said.

Garth was still groggy, but he immediately said to me, "The spread, Annie, the spread." He pointed down to his legs.

I looked where he pointed, but could only see the sheet covering his legs. "What is it, sweetheart?"

"The spread," he said again.

I lifted the sheet and saw what he was talking about. They had his legs separated and immobilized so he couldn't move his operated on hip. I could see that this was putting pressure on his left hip, which we knew now probably had been weakened by cancer as well.

"Are you in pain, sweetheart?"

He nodded. "It's the spread."

I tried to explain what Garth was complaining about to the people bustling around in the room, but they were not focusing on me. I decided to try and find Garth's doctor. At the nurses' station I told them I needed to speak with the doctor. They managed to get him on the phone. I explained the problem to him and said Garth needed the separation of his legs to be decreased. The doctor talked with a nurse, who went in and adjusted Garth's legs a little.

I told them I planned to stay the night. They brought in a rollaway bed for me.

When everyone was gone, Garth was falling asleep. He looked up at me through drooping eyes.

"Annie, are you staying?"

I nodded. "Is the spread better?"

"A little."

He closed his eyes.

I pulled my bed up close to his and lay down. Though I felt relieved that he had made it through the surgery, I still felt scared. He seemed so fragile, so small. How was he going to make it back from this? The peace I felt at having him here and being here with him felt tentative, vulnerable, like the first rays of sun after a violent storm. There were still some very dark clouds in the sky that threatened another deluge at any moment.

———

In the summer of 1984, we were gathered for Garth's and my nuptials. Under one roof were myself and Garth; my first husband, Dave, and his wife Clare; Rose; and my mother. Because my mother had never forgiven Dave for our divorce, the arrangements provided a tense backdrop to the happy occasion. My mother did not understand Dave's and my ongoing friendship.

I felt very happy and had not allowed the tension in the house or the stress of preparations to affect me to the point that when my mother asked if I had ordered a cake, I admitted it had slipped my mind. Mother took care of this oversight.

The day was sunny and warm. We all gathered at a friend's house for the ceremony. Garth and I were into New Age spirituality at the time and had a teacher from Paramahansa Yogananda's tradition presiding. We wrote the proceedings ourselves, which were unique enough to cause Garth's 90 year old nearly deaf Uncle Pine to think he had stumbled onto some kind of cult.

At one point I planned to give Dave a rose to recognize him and what our relationship had meant to me. I prepared a short speech about how I had come to understand getting married a second time not so much as a failure, but as an expansion—Dave and I were still friends and we now included Garth and Clare in our circle of intimacy. I had also planned to give roses to my mother, the only parent present, to represent Garth's and my gratitude to our parents. I began to cry before I could explain any of this and Garth had to rescue me and try to explain my rose ritual.

It brought a tear to Dave's eyes, but my mother, a fundamental Christian, standing there in this circle with all our friends, participating in a ceremony she did not understand, seemed to take the roses that Garth and I presented to her as a slight, as if she were being singled out for some kind of punishment.

A few days later, on the Fourth of July, we were having a barbecue out in the yard. Again, this gathering was attended by this uncomfortable grouping of the newlyweds, Rose, my mother, Dave and Clare, and a couple other friends.

At some point, it was suggested that we should sing the national anthem, since it was the Fourth. Several people stood with their hands over their hearts, others of us simply joined in. Clare, who was taking issue with nationalism in those days as the root of a lot of our world's ills, refused to participate.

My mother glared across the picnic table at Clare. When dinner was done, Mom disappeared to her room and Rose came out to warn me that she was packing.

I found Mom in her room. I could almost see steam rising from her body.

"What are you doing, Mom?" I asked.

"I'm going home! No one wants me here! I'm leaving!"

Part of me knew this was about my mother being in a foreign land she did not understand. Her daughter had just done something in someone's house that didn't represent any kind of marriage ceremony she could recall. She was in the same house with her former hated son-in-law and his unpatriotic spouse. And no one as near as she could tell was Christian. She had had enough.

"Mom," I said, "I want you here. Garth wants you here. Rose wants you here."

She maintained her pouting demeanor.

"Besides, you can't go now. You'll miss the fireworks. You were so looking forward to them."

I saw a flicker of interest in her face.

"Why don't we forget about this for now and just go enjoy the fireworks? We can talk about it later if you want."

She seemed to agree reluctantly, but I also sensed some relief. She was in a world she did not understand, but she wanted to see the fireworks, and she did like this Garth, her daughter's new husband.

7

After Garth's hip surgery we were faced with getting him back on his feet so we could get to radiation therapy for his other hip, which we now knew also had cancer in it. This involved physical therapy a couple times a week by professionals and the rest of the time with my help. I was now doing everything for Garth and myself. I had begun to feel the weight of my responsibility.

On April 14 I woke up feeling angry. I felt so isolated in this battle, as if Garth's survival depended on me alone. Garth's hospital bed was in the living room and I was sleeping on the couch nearby so I could help him during the night as needed. I was in the kitchen fixing coffee when Garth said from his bed, where he was propped up on pillows, "Annie, I want to try and start working again at the store. Maybe you could get some things for me so I could work on a couple projects."

I felt enraged at this request. I snapped at him, "I don't think I can do one more thing, Garth."

He looked frustrated and hurt. I went upstairs to the bathroom to be alone and cool down. I sat on the toilet with my head in my hands feeling how enormous the tasks of daily life had become. A noise like an animal howl came from somewhere — I thought it was the neighbor's cat.

But as I descended the stairs, I saw what the noise had been. Garth was having convulsions in the bed. Sheer terror drew me to his side at a run. I grabbed him by the shoulders and yelled at him, "You can't leave me, Garth! You can't leave me!" His body stopped convulsing, but he remained unconscious. I hugged his body to me as I said, "Sweetheart, I love you. You can't leave!"

Somehow I realized Garth had had a seizure. I thought he was dying because he was mad at me. Panic guided me to pick up the phone and dial 911. A voice on the other end of the line tried to evaluate my situation, "Is he conscious?"

"No," I said loudly. "He's not convulsing anymore, but he's not conscious."

"Try lowering his head. Can you do that?"

I gently removed all the pillows so that Garth's head sunk down into the bed. He started to come around just as the medics arrived. I hung up the phone. Garth looked from me to the emergency personnel surrounding him. "You brought people here?" he asked with irritation.

One woman asked me, "What's wrong with him?"

"He has cancer."

"Is he in the last stages?" she asked.

It felt almost like an attack, an affront. "No, he isn't," I said firmly, almost defensively.

It was decided he needed to go to emergency. Later that day we discovered that the cancer had now invaded Garth's brain. When the doctors asked us if we wanted radiation to treat it, we said of course. Garth stayed overnight in the hospital for observation. The next day a physical therapist helped us learn how to get him into the car, which we hadn't been able to do since his surgery, so I could take him home and then bring him back for radiation.

We started the daily trips to radiation to treat both his left hip and brain. I had moved into a new place with Garth's care since the seizure. Though we never discussed it, I began to feel his vulnerability, how fragile his life had become. My fear helped me to drop my anger and resentment at how burdensome our life had been feeling. All I wanted was for Garth to get better.

The first day of radiation, after I wheeled him into the radiation room, one of the technicians started to transfer Garth from the wheelchair to a gurney for the radiation. He quickly swung Garth's legs up onto the gurney and I saw Garth wince. I jumped in front of the technician and took over the job. I snapped at him, "Be careful!" When Garth was arranged on the gurney I said to the technicians standing around, "Come get me when you're done and I'll help him get back into his wheelchair." They didn't argue with me.

So each day at home I would help him into the car, help him out of the car at the hospital, wheel him into radiation, help him up onto the gurney for the treatment, come back after the radiation to help him back into the wheelchair, help him back into the car to go home, wheel him back into the house and help him back to bed when we got home. It exhausted us both.

We never discussed what this metastasis to the brain meant. We kept trying to decide what the next treatment would be. I researched a tea called Essiac, acquired some, and began fixing it for Garth. My brother told us about a new vaccine and Garth asked his doctor to check it out.

Yet the struggle began to wear us down. I no longer felt angry, but I was so tired. One day Garth grabbed the trapeze above his bed and said through gritted teeth, "I hate this! Why don't you just shoot me?"

I went to his side. "Are you in pain, sweetheart?"

"I'm always in pain!"

I began the routine of adjusting his pillows to try and make him more comfortable. But we just couldn't seem to get him into a position where neither hip hurt or where a worrisome sore on his coccyx that had developed didn't bother him. "Annie, I can't stand this! I hate this!" he seemed near tears. "And now you're even tired of me!" He thrust it at me like an accusation.

I looked at Garth. The pain in his face and voice broke my heart. I felt my own exhaustion. "Sweetheart, I am tired," I admitted. "I am not tired of you."

Something drained out of Garth's tense face, leaving only pain. A kind of relief enveloped us both as he said softly, "You are so good to me, Annie."

Rose came for a week to help out and took over the job of taking Garth to radiation so I could try to catch up at work. One day while they waited for Garth's turn in the radiation chamber, he said to her, "Rose, I'm scared. I feel like I'm on the edge." Just then the door opened and they were summoned for his treatment. Rose could not bring herself to ask Garth about this later.

Dave came for a week to help out and sat me down next to Garth's bed in the living room one evening. "Have you guys talked about what Garth wants at this point if he has a heart attack or something?"

I looked at Garth and away. I could not stand the look of resignation and loss of hope in his eyes.

"I don't want heroics," he said.

Dave pressed on, "What about if you die from this, Garth? Do you know what you want after?"

Part of me hated Dave for asking these questions even while I was grateful. I looked at Garth and he looked at me almost as if he believed I had put Dave up to this. I felt like a traitor for even listening to his response.

"You mean do I want to be buried?"

"Yes," said Dave.

"I guess cremated," Garth said.

We couldn't stand more and I got up and went into the kitchen. Later Dave told me that the swelling in Garth's legs probably indicated congestive heart failure and that could be how Garth would die. I listened, but didn't respond.

I was in some kind of strange world of denial that protected me from reality even while I prepared for what was becoming inevitable. Dave had given me *The Tibetan Book of Living and Dying* some months previously. I had been practicing several techniques from that book. One was tonglen, a practice for easing the suffering of others. The other was a phowa practice for helping someone who is dying transcend.

The home health nurses that came several times a week to tend to Garth's now serious wound on his coccyx began to mention Hospice every visit. "That means we have to admit Garth is terminal, doesn't it?" I asked. They agreed this was true. "We do not believe that," I said.

So the nurses kept coming.

The morning of June 7, I called Garth's doctor and asked for a home visit. I wanted the doctor to see Garth and perhaps offer him some relief for his swollen legs and feet, his now distended belly, and his shortness of breath.

The nurse I talked to said the doctor would come. Then, she asked me, "Annie, you know Garth is dying don't you?"

Tears sprung into my eyes and I said almost defiantly, "No, I don't!"

When I hung up I cried to Garth, "Sweetheart, she says you're dying!"

Garth looked at me and then away, "She doesn't know," he said.

I felt an absurd relief, like somehow this was in Garth's control.

A home health nurse arrived to tend to Garth's wound. He now had several more sores on his hips and legs that they were bandaging as well.

I helped the nurse turn Garth on his side so she could change the dressing on his coccyx. When she uncovered the wound, she looked at me and shook her head. The wound had evidently gotten much worse. I hugged Garth's head to me for comfort, as much for myself as for him.

After the nurse left, one of the bandages on another wound came loose. As I tried to remove it for a repair, Garth's skin came off into my hand. Horror invaded every fiber of my being as I tried to patch it back on. A cold hard sliver of fear slipped next to my heart.

The doctor arrived about seven p.m. I told him about my concerns and that the nurses had suggested small doses of morphine to address Garth's shortness of breath. The doctor wrote out a prescription. As he handed it to me, he asked, "What do you both think of this situation?"

I looked at Garth and he looked at me. "What do you think, Annie?" he said.

"I know the situation is very grave," I admitted. "But I haven't given up hope."

The doctor turned to Garth. "I don't think you're going to beat this thing," he said.

I began to realize the cross purposes of this visit. I had brought the doctor here to try and get Garth some relief for his symptoms. Garth had hoped the doctor would tell him how he was going to help him survive. The doctor had come to tell us Garth was going to die.

The doctor convinced us to allow Hospice to come in by telling us if Garth got better, we could tell them to leave. Then he left.

Garth seemed exhausted by this visit. I felt fear at what had just transpired.

"Garth," I said, "What do you think about bringing in Hospice?" I knew he wouldn't want everyone to start coming around to tell him goodbye.

Garth was slipping toward sleep. He seemed barely able to keep his eyes open. Suddenly, I felt panic invading me.

"Garth," I said with some urgency. "You're not going tonight are you?"

He opened his eyes briefly and flung a terse, "No," in my direction as if he were swatting a fly.

I tried to get him to take some of the Essiac tea, but he shook his head. I tried to help him brush his teeth, but he pushed the toothbrush away.

He was drifting off quickly now, but he opened his eyes briefly and held mine as he mouthed the words, "I love you, Annie." There was a finality to his words that frightened me, but I pushed the feeling away. I let him go to sleep. I was exhausted myself and was asleep as soon as I lay down on the couch next to his bed.

———

In the spring of 1983, Garth and I were living temporarily with Rose in her California apartment. We had moved there from Oregon in search of more stable employment. I was driving for a company that provided transportation to the elderly and Garth was working in a natural foods store. I had read a book on "spiritual birth control" and we were practicing this birth control method, which consisted of mentally attuning to all possible birthing beings before each sexual act and alerting them to the fact that *now* was *not* the appropriate time for conception.

We had been practicing this method for over a year, so I was surprised when it failed in March. I was sure it was Garth who had fallen down on the spiritual birth control job. We never discussed the possibility of not having this child, however, but simply moved toward preparing for its arrival. We decided we would quit our jobs in June and look for an appropriate place to raise our little girl. Garth was certain the baby would be a girl and he had already named her Amanda. He said, "She's going to have curly hair like you, Annie."

The day after I quit my job, we were on a walk in the neighborhood around our apartment, when I felt some contractions. We quickly headed back home. Garth called our doctor's office while I went into the bathroom and discovered a little blood.

I came back out to the couch and lay down.

Garth turned from the phone. "Are you okay?"

"There's blood," I said.

He told the nurse about my blood. When he hung up, he came to sit beside me. "They said you should stay in bed for a couple days." He looked scared.

I knew Garth wasn't at all sure about this baby idea. I wasn't either. We weren't even married. Yet, we already felt like parents. Garth had been exhibiting both nervousness and excitement about our impending birth. He had told most people we knew, even though I was barely three months along.

I went to bed early. I still felt as if my period was about to start.

In the middle of the night I woke with intense pain. I felt my insides were about to burst and ran into the bathroom. Just as I got to the toilet, blood came gushing out of me. Garth ran after me as I sat there with my head in my hands. I was crying. "I'm sorry, Garth. I lost our baby. I'm sorry," I cried.

Garth knelt beside me. "Annie, you didn't lose our baby."

I kept crying and apologizing. "You were so excited, Garth. I'm sorry. I feel I've failed you."

"Annie, don't be ridiculous! This isn't your fault!"

The absolute certainty in his voice drew my eyes up to his face. "You're not upset with me?"

"Upset with you?" He looked at me with incredulity. He hugged me to him. "Let's get you back to bed," he said.

The next few days I stayed in bed and Garth tended to my needs. He made me soup and got me fresh carrot and wheat grass juice. He called our doctor to find out what I needed to do to make sure I would be okay. I felt some sadness at what might have been, but Garth's loving care brought new warmth for him into my heart. We had lost Amanda, but we had found a new tenderness between us.

8

At a little after one in the morning, a noise woke me. I sat up on the couch and looked over at Garth. His left arm was flung out toward the side table and he was breathing strange. I went to his side. I put his arm back under the covers. Though Garth's breathing was gentler, I recognized it as similar to what my father had done just before he died. It was the first time since his seizure that he had been unconscious.

For some reason, I felt calm. I did not even think about calling 911. I recognized the end and felt peaceful and even a kind of relief for both of us. I sat down next to Garth's bed.

"Garth, you can go now. Sweetheart, you've suffered enough. It's okay, my love, you can go."

Part of me sat apart from this, watching in amazement. I was telling Garth he could go? Who was telling Garth he could go?

The other calmer part began to do the phowa meditation I had been practicing for months. I visualized Garth rising above his body and meeting Padmasambhava above in the sky. I tried to hold that vision.

The minutes trudged forward. I got up to go upstairs to the bathroom and told Garth where I was going. When I got back, he was much the same. I knew he wouldn't want to be in this state long. I told him again that he could go. I felt sad, but I didn't feel alone. Garth was here in the room and so was something else. Some kind of acceptance. A willingness. Resignation?

So this was how it was going to end. With Garth and I in a room alone. I supposed he had chosen this. I supposed he had known somehow he couldn't go on anymore and didn't want strangers from Hospice coming. Didn't want family and friends coming to say goodbye.

I felt so much love for Garth, yet I also felt relief. Guilt tugged at my consciousness. How could you feel relief? What kind of person are you? That critical voice made me cringe.

The minutes became hours. I began to feel weary about four in the morning. I wondered how long this was going to take. Garth remained unconscious doing that soft struggled breathing. It occurred to me for a moment that I could hasten this. I could end it somehow. It was only me here.

Horror filled me at what I had just contemplated. How could I entertain such a possibility for one second? I must be a terrible person. This was Garth! I decided to lay down a moment and went to the couch.

Shame invaded me as I lay there. I cringed to think what I had just contemplated. I thought about what a shallow person I had often been in my life. I wanted to be different. I wanted to change who I was. I no longer wanted to be so self focused; so caught up in all my personal bullshit. I wanted to be a better person. I wanted to be able to help others.

I thought of Garth lying there dying. I wanted him to be able to go quickly. I didn't want him to suffer anymore. I called out in my heart and mind to Padmasambhava, "Help Garth, Padmasambhava! Please, I beg you to help Garth!" Tears sprung to my eyes.

Immediately Garth's breathing changed. I got up and went to his side. Each breath seemed to be getting more shallow than the last. I began to do the phowa for him again. As I sat there by Garth's side visualizing him rising to meet Padmasambhava in the air above his bed, ever so gently he let out his final breath and I heard or felt a kind of "whoosh." Then he was still.

I sat for a few moments overwhelmed and astounded at the look in Garth's eyes. They were wide open now, gazing upwards with awe, as if he had seen something wonderful. I felt an unspeakable peace just to look at him.

"Sweetheart," I said, "you are so beautiful. God's speed, sweetheart." I felt his release as if it was my own. It was 4:47 a.m.

At about five a.m. I called Rose. Though Rose always turned her phone off at night, for some reason she had woken early this morning and turned it on. As she was getting married in three days, she couldn't come right away. She said she would let the rest of the family know. I called Dave and Clare. Dave said he would come at once. He left the phone to begin his preparations and Clare told me she would come after Rose's wedding. I called Garth's Dad. He would let Garth's brothers know.

I hung up the phone. Now I felt alone. I called my neighbor, Sally, and asked her to come over. I knew I wanted to keep Garth's body for 24 hours as is suggested in the *Tibetan Book of Living and Dying*. This would hopefully give Garth's spirit time to fully separate from his body.

Sally arrived. She seemed stunned and bereft. I still felt a kind of unearthly calm. I asked her to practice the phowa for Garth with me and explained it to her. We sat for a few minutes by his bed in silence doing this practice.

After a few minutes, Sally suggested, "Let's go outside."

We went out on the deck and looked across the field in back. I could tell Sally didn't know what to say or do and felt awkward. I still felt this peace that seemed so in contrast to what had just happened. We went back inside and went to Garth's side.

"His mouth!" Sally said with surprise.

When we had gone outside, Garth's mouth had been slightly open. Now it was almost entirely closed into a half smile. The combination of the awed look in his eyes and that half smile comforted me tremendously. I felt soothed that he seemed to be finally at peace. "I bet he was glad to get out of that body," I said.

Sally just looked at me and back at Garth without a word. She seemed nonplused.

I kept feeling drawn to look at Garth often during the next 24 hours. Whenever I'd start to feel bad, I would go and look at him and immediately feel better. I kept telling him how much I loved him and how beautiful he was. I told him how much I appreciated his gentle going and that when he knew it was over he went quickly.

Dave arrived by noon and Sally left. He began answering the phone and making arrangements for a memorial service. He made arrangements for Garth's body to be taken the next morning.

That night I started out sleeping on the couch near Garth's body. I didn't want to leave him alone. Dave slept in our bed upstairs.

I woke in the middle of the night and went upstairs to the bathroom. When I came out of the bathroom, I couldn't bring myself to go back downstairs. I went into the bedroom where Dave slept. He woke when I approached the bed.

"Can I get in here?" I asked.

He made room for me and I crawled in next to him.

In the morning when I woke, Dave was already in the bathroom. I got up and got dressed. Dave came out of the bathroom and I went in. When I came out, Dave was in the bedroom.

I went in to him. "Dave, I'm a little nervous about going downstairs."

He looked at me from where he had been putting something in his suitcase. "Me too."

"I'm not certain how he'll look after all this time."

Dave nodded. "Yeah. Look, I'll go down first."

"Are you sure?"

He nodded and headed down the stairs. Shortly, he called up to me, "Annie, he's fine. Hasn't changed much."

I went down and sure enough he looked about the same. He still had that awed expression in his eyes and that half smile. I felt relieved. I touched his arm. It was cold.

"They'll be here soon to take him, Annie."

"Will you help me tell Garth to make sure and leave his body before they come?"

So Dave and I sat next to Garth's body to say goodbye. The tears came as I said, "You need to leave your body now, Sweetheart. They're coming to take it. I love you with all my heart. You will never be forgotten."

Two men arrived promptly at nine o'clock. I had to sign some papers. I could tell they were trying to be gentle. But when they pulled out a bag to put Garth in I said, "I can't watch this."

"I'll stay and watch them do this, Annie, you go outside," said Dave.

"Are you sure?"

"Yes."

I went out on the deck and then down the steps into the field behind. The tears began to come. The immensity of what had just occurred began to engulf me. Dave came outside after a few minutes and sat beside me.

"They were very respectful, Annie, in the way they took him."

I looked at Dave. "Thank you for staying with him, Dave."

He took me in his arms and we sat there in the field holding each other and cried.

———

In the summer of 1981 Garth asked my friend, Priscilla, and I to go to Umpqua Hot Springs with him and his buddy, Mick. I was involved with another man at the time, Jake, and Jake was furious that I had accepted this invitation that included camping overnight. I suppose it was kind of odd, but this was the '80s. Priscilla and I seemed not to think of it as an overnight date, or we pretended to be naive. We knew the guys were probably interested in us, but even pretended not to know who was interested in whom, even though Priscilla was probably seven or eight inches taller than Garth.

We went in Garth's 52 Ford pickup, taking turns up front and in the back. We were lucky to have the hot springs to ourselves, a large dug out hole in the earth creating a pool for many people to share. I looked at both men in the water opposite Priscilla and I, wondering. Garth was a very small man, probably only 5' 3". He had brown soft hair that fell down over his forehead. His body was brown, as if he had lain in the sun that summer. His smile and his laugh were both nervous and warm. His friend, Mick, was tall and slim with blond hair. We all smiled at each other that first time in the hot springs, a little embarrassed at our nakedness.

Later that afternoon, Garth asked me to go on a walk with him. We left Mick and Priscilla and headed off into the forest. It was a hot summer day, but the trees were cooling. It reminded me of back East in summer, though it wasn't near so humid. But the languidness, the heat, the forest, and the summer carefreeness were reminiscent of my childhood.

"So you're from Virginia," said Garth.

"Yeah, mug city in the summer. God I remember those hot summers. We used to drip sweat in our beds."

"Upper New York could be like that too," he said. "We had forest in back of our house in Chappaqua. I spent my whole summer outdoors."

We wandered on through the forest talking lazily of childhoods and families and our pasts. At one point we sat down together in the woods next to a small stream. I watched the stream, lost in thought. Garth plucked a blade of grass and held it between his hands, blowing on it. It took him several tries until he got the blade of grass to quiver with his breath just so. A soft low noise was emitted like a horn. He blew on the blade several times, creating that horn-like call.

The noise turned my attention to Garth and I looked at him as if seeing him for the first time. Suddenly I realized that I was sitting next to a man in the forest who had just made a blade of grass sing.

He picked a fresh blade. "Here," he said. "You try."

But I only created squeaks and buzzes and slobbered on my hands. We laughed at my efforts and he demonstrated again. The soft low call touched me in a way no words could have done. I looked into his hazel eyes and smiled. He looked back at me smiling. It was an introduction.

9

In Tibetan Buddhist tradition, it is believed that the spirit of the person who has died goes through a process of separation for up to 49 days before moving on. During that time their spirit is supposedly very affected by the actions and thoughts of those they have left behind.

Though I didn't know if this was true, I was doing the phowa practice regularly for Garth, hoping it would help him. Rose stayed with me for two weeks after his death, even though she had just gotten married, and this meant she had to forego her honeymoon.

Rose had told me that during her wedding ceremony, she faced the crowd and explained why Garth and I could not be there.

"People told me afterwards, Annie, that while I spoke about Garth, a butterfly landed in my hair."

I didn't know quite what to make of that or the sensations I was having of Garth's presence. It seemed when I felt particularly bad, I would feel this presence all around me.

Rose was writing thank you notes to family and friends for wedding gifts during her stay. One day I was in the kitchen fixing coffee while Rose sat at the table by the sliding glass doors to the deck. Though the hospital bed was gone, I could still see Garth lying there in my mind's eye. Then I saw Rose sitting at the table with a half smile on her face while she penned notes about her recent nuptials.

The juxtaposition of Rose's happiness with my devastation and loss collided in my brain like a musical dissonance. I almost wanted to shatter Rose's happiness somehow. While she sat there with love's new bloom, my heart shuddered from the blow it had received. The stark contrast brought the full force of the present moment into my consciousness. As the coffee dripped, I looked outside. The cedar at the edge of the deck looked a deeper green than I remembered and the sky filtering through its branches, a deeper blue.

After Rose left, Dave and Clare came to stay with me. We headed up to Mount Hood to camp for a few days. We pulled into McNeil campground, where Garth and I had camped many times. As Dave and Clare set up their tent, I began putting up Garth's and my tent for the first time alone. I could almost see him stooping down to help me thread the poles that now resisted my efforts. I could see him on the other side of the fly as we lifted it in place. I could not manage this tent-raising task on my own and had to ask for help. Dave came, but it wasn't easy, like the rhythm Garth and I had learned through the years. Having someone else struggle with me to put up this tent only made his absence sharper.

When we sat down to dinner, the empty spot where Garth should have been felt like a black hole. I felt sucked into it, unable to enjoy being in the woods with my friends. As we cleaned up and dusk began to settle around us, I heard a familiar call followed by a whooshing sound. I looked up to see a nighthawk in the sky. I grabbed my binoculars to be sure, then said to Dave and Clare, "Hey guys, nighthawks."

Dave and Clare got their binocs and trained them up to where I pointed. There were several now, darting up and down in their noisy display.

"What did you say they are, Annie?" asked Dave.

"Common nighthawks," I answered, still watching them through my binocs.

"Cool," he said.

We watched the little flock it had become now until they flew off to another part of the forest.

"Boy, that was neat!" said Dave. His enthusiasm and excitement were contagious and I felt a small glimmer of the old simple joy I used to feel at just seeing a cool bird in the sky. "I've never seen those birds before, Annie. They're great!" exclaimed Dave.

I nodded and smiled. The glimmer was fading fast as I began to feel divorced from the excitement Dave and Clare were sharing. I recognized how they were feeling, but I could not go there, not now, perhaps never again. Not when everything about my world felt empty and wrong. The pain in my heart was like a blanket over my mind. I could not see the world's beauty the way I used to through my shroud of darkness.

The next day I led Dave and Clare on the hike to Ramona Falls, which they had never done. The day was crisp and clean. Dave waxed almost poetic with his praise of the astounding sheet of water, the rainbow-colored rock walls, the gurgling playful stream, and the sparkling forest. I felt happy for him that he could appreciate the beauty, almost as if I was an observer watching a film. I could see his happiness, I could almost be warmed by it, but it was not mine. The wound that had been opened in my heart was not being touched by nature's healing balm. It felt like a dagger had been thrust into my heart and yanked out without caution. I was left with this gaping hole that swallowed everything else until all that was left was aching, unrelenting, sharp pain.

Clare had to return to California to her job, but since it was summer, Dave had some time off from his job as a Unitarian Minister. He stayed with me for another week.

He asked me the morning Clare left what he could help me with. I told him I didn't need both our vehicles and planned to just keep our car. I wanted to donate the Toyota pickup in Garth's name to the Red Cross to help the people in Rwanda.

"Garth was particularly concerned about the Rwandan people," I told him. "And I'd like to donate Garth's leftover medications and supplies to somebody."

"Okay, Annie," said Dave. "Why don't you go clean out the truck? I'll make the arrangements."

So I went out to our pickup and began going through it. I couldn't believe that tears flowed even during this mundane activity as I sorted through the stuffed glove compartment. I was relieved to be getting rid of the truck as it had chronic problems and felt like a burden to me now. I was so glad I had convinced Garth that we ought to buy the new Honda Civic just a couple years previously. He had been hesitant, having never purchased a new car before. But after we'd had it a few months, he had already begun to talk about an upgrade. I told him we should stick with what we had for awhile.

As I got to the back of the glove compartment, I saw the old wooden shrunken head Garth kept there. It had been his father's and Garth had said it was a lucky charm to protect our travels. For some reason it was this memento that I had always thought hideous, that caused me to sit there in the passenger's seat of our old truck shedding tears in a sudden torrent. I held the ugly wooden head in my hand as if it were something precious and cried until I couldn't cry anymore.

When I was finally able to finish the task at hand, I went back inside the house. Dave had made arrangements for the truck to be picked up the next day. He had also found out we could take the medications and supplies to a local AIDS hospice.

Later that week, Dave and I went for a hike in the Gorge. We stopped at one point and I complained of sore feet. Dave took my shoes off and began rubbing the offending appendages. A passerby expressed envy at such luck. "She deserves it," said Dave.

I knew the stranger probably thought we were a couple. I was struck in that moment with the oddness of the situation. Here I was on a hike with my former husband shortly after my current husband had died. And this former husband was rubbing my feet. What was the likelihood of that?

I think it was on this hike that Dave told me he was having some kind of bladder difficulty and thought he should see a doctor. We went together to this doctor's visit. This trip to the doctors had an eerie quality for me as I sat in the waiting room. When Dave came out, I steeled myself against his news. But all he said was they thought he had a bladder infection and had given him an antibiotic. He seemed relieved and I realized we both had been expecting the worst. Leaving that doctor's waiting room felt like an escape from some kind of suffocation.

———

One winter in the late 80's, Garth and I drove to Bend in our '78 Toyota pickup to meet Rose, Dave, and Clare for a few days of skiing. The night after we all arrived, the thermometer in Bend dropped out of sight. We woke our first morning to temperatures at 30 degrees below zero. We all tentatively began to get ready to head up skiing. After loading our equipment into the truck, Garth and I got in it while everyone else got in Dave's car. Garth was at the steering wheel. When he turned the ignition, there was a slight shudder and then nothing.

"It's froze, Annie," he said.

We got out and Garth went to look under the hood, while I went over to Dave's car, which was purring unconcernedly. Dave rolled down his window.

"Our truck won't start," I said. "Seems to be frozen." Clare and Rose peered at me behind Dave's head.

Dave got out of his car and went with me back to the truck. Garth was still looking under the hood.

Garth looked up at us. "I think she's frozen solid. Did yours start?" he asked Dave.

"Took a few cranks, but she's going."

"I'm freezing," I commented.

"Let's go back to the room and decide what to do," suggested Dave.

As Garth let our truck's hood down, Dave went to get Rose and Clare. Garth and I retreated to inside warmth.

Once inside, I said, "You know, I think it's too cold to ski anyway."

"Yeah," Garth sounded disappointed. "But we better try to get the truck going."

Rose and Clare arrived while I was on the phone with Triple A. The harassed voice on the other end of the line said they'd had so many calls they probably wouldn't get to us for a couple days if at all. I hung up.

"They're not going to be any help," I told Garth.

"I guess we're not going skiing, huh?" asked Rose.

Clare shivered. "It's too cold anyway."

"Where's Dave?" I asked.

"He saw a guy in the parking lot helping someone get their car started and went over to check it out," said Clare.

Dave showed up a few minutes later. His face was red from the cold. "Hey, there's a guy out there with a heater. He's helping people get their cars started. I think he'll help us if we kind of hang out there letting him know we need help."

"You guys don't have to get involved in our truck problem, Dave. Maybe you all would like to go do something fun," I suggested.

"Hey, your truck problem is our problem, Annie. I'll go back out in a few minutes and hang around that guy. I need to get warmed up first."

"I'll go now," Garth said.

So Garth and Dave took turns keeping our need in the Good Samaritan's mind, while Rose, Clare, and I fixed some food.

By early afternoon, they had achieved the benefactor's help and he had his heater sitting under our truck's hood. We got the truck started some time later and drove to Les Schwab to have the battery checked. They said we could leave our truck inside their shop that night.

We decided to go out to dinner before we headed home from our aborted trip the next day. We couldn't wait to get out of that deep freeze.

We parked in downtown Bend and rushed from our car toward the warmth of the restaurant. Dave and Clare were a few yards ahead of Garth, Rose, and I. There was a man sitting on the sidewalk next to the door of the restaurant. I was wondering with a tinge of horror if he was homeless when I saw Dave stoop and speak to him. Then Dave handed the man something. The man seemed to nod vaguely.

As we followed Dave and Clare into the restaurant, we passed the man, who still sat on the sidewalk. His eyes were almost slits, as he seemed to steel himself against the cold. He didn't look at us. I shuddered to think of him having no place to go.

Inside the restaurant, we found Dave and Clare seated at a table. I looked at Dave. "Is that man homeless, Dave?"

He shrugged; his face grimaced with concern. "Sure looks like it."

"Did you give him money?"

"I didn't know what else to do. He can't survive out there. I gave him 20 dollars and told him to get inside somewhere."

I felt some relief. It seemed unclear if the man would be able to marshal himself even with that succor, but at least Dave had tried. I felt grateful to him. I felt privileged at that moment that Dave was my friend. I had been worried about the man, but I'm not sure I would have done anything about it. I was so relieved and grateful and even a little surprised that Dave had.

10

After Dave left, I was alone. There was nothing now between me and the emptiness. There was nothing I wanted to do. Nothing I was interested in. I quit my job where Garth and I had worked. I couldn't stand the thought of entering that place alone, trying to do the newsletter we had done together.

One day as I walked the streets of my neighborhood, the weight of my grief bore down on me. I noticed the colors of the trees and sky. I felt present to them, saw their beauty, but the brightness and deep blue were no balm to me. The sharp pain in my heart brought tears to cloud my eyes. I could not believe this had happened. I could not believe Garth was gone. How could he be gone so completely? Where was he?

The tears became a torrent and I had to sit down on a nearby curb. My body shook with the force of my inner storm. In the world outside it was sunny and the sky was calm. I was perplexed by the contrast. How could my world be so utterly torn asunder and the outer world continue as before?

It seemed unreal. I felt disconnected from the normalcy around me. There was a dissonance sounding into my depths, yet the sun continued to shine. I sat on the curb as the desolation overwhelmed me. How could I go on? What was to become of me? I missed Garth so terribly.

I struggled to my feet. I felt almost unable to walk. I tried to remember how far it was back home. Could I make it? How would I get help if I could not make it?

You can put one foot in front of the other, I suggested to myself. I started. It seemed I would never get back home and no one seemed to be around in the entire neighborhood. I felt utterly alone, caught in the tangles of my sorrow. I rounded another corner. How far was it now? I could not remember. The tears had stopped momentarily, but not the pain. The pain radiated from my heart into my very soul.

I wondered if I would die before I could make it home. When the long driveway leading to my house finally came into view, I wasn't relieved; I still wasn't sure I would make it. Finally inside the house, I collapsed on the couch as the tears started again. Could one cry oneself to death? I had not known one person had so much water in them.

In the next weeks, I began to see a therapist. I recognized that I could not navigate this barren terrain alone. The therapist, Nancy, helped guide the raging torrent inside me that threatened to overwhelm the banks of my sanity.

Garth's cousin, Julie, wrote me an e-mail telling me how much her son had cared for Garth. I sent her an e-mail back hinting at how I feared Garth's death would be my undoing. She began a daily e-mail contact.

In the fall, I began grief classes. The instructor, Janet, had lost her husband, and described a day she spent, curled into a tight ball in a corner of her house, unable to move. I knew by the way Janet looked into my eyes that she'd felt my same searing anguish. Janet told us we needed to say goodbye to our loved one in a series of rituals. I heard her words, but what really touched me that first night was the realization of her knowing. She knew what this was like. I felt such relief to know I wasn't the only one who had ever experienced such shattering sorrow.

Yet, I wondered if I was cracking up. Nothing had prepared me for this intensity of pain that I literally did not know if I could survive. Every morning when I woke to a world without Garth, I had to relive the horror of emptiness and loss. I just could not understand my strange and lonely new life.

In October, Dave called me. He didn't beat around the bush. "Annie," he said, "I have some bad news."

I held my breath.

"They've found cancer in my prostate."

"Dave," I managed, "that's terrible."

"I know. But they think it's treatable. This isn't a death sentence."

I had heard that before. I tried to say some encouraging words before I hung up the phone.

What was happening? What had I done wrong? What was happening to my world?

———

In the spring of 1979, Dave and I were living in Ashland. He was in nursing school and I was supporting us by working at the college. We had moved there from California the previous summer so Dave could enter school.

From the start of this new phase, we began to have trouble again. Being surrounded by other women all day long did not help Dave remain firm in his monogamous resolve. Though I knew he was struggling inside, I was surprised by his decision that he shared with me on a long walk out at Emigrant Lake.

It was a sunny day, but cool. We had driven out to the lake in the afternoon in our aging Ford Maverick. Dave's hair was golden in those days and he was clean-shaven, except for a curly red mustache. We were both in flannel shirts and jeans. Our sheltie, Brummel, ran ahead of us on the path.

Dave was quiet beside me and I sensed he had come to some decision, but I thought his decision had gone the other way. We were walking along, when he finally spoke, "Annie," he said, "I think we need to separate."

I looked at him, unbelieving. He was Dave, my husband. His red and gold shrouded head flashed at me before I turned away. I felt as if he had hit me. I didn't know what to say; how to stop him.

"I'm sorry, Annie."

"Dave," I managed, "I think you're making a mistake."

I could feel him grimace beside me. "This isn't easy, Annie, I know. But I think it is the only way."

How could he do this? How could I stop him? Brummel stood in the middle of the path ahead of us looking back, as if to say, "Hey, what's going on?"

Dave began to talk about his plan, how he would move out of our house and into an apartment. I heard his words, but they seemed far away. I felt as if a permanent bond had been forged between us. Dave was tugging hard at it. Could he sever that bond just by deciding to? I did not know how to change what had been enough to hold him.

As we walked back up toward the car, a heaviness settled on my heart. Brummel walked right next to us, instead of running ahead, looking up at us expectantly.

11

By February I was getting regular therapy from Nancy and beginning to learn about ritual from Janet. I decided to attend a retreat in Seattle with a student of Sogyal Rinpoche on grief and loss. It had been Rinpoche's book that had helped me access help from Padmasambhava at the moment of Garth's death. I was just beginning to be able to share my experience with others and had started to understand sharing's healing properties.

The retreat felt large to me with about 75 people in attendance. I sat in my chair in the big conference room doing the exercises and crying. At one point the teacher talked about doing the phowa for someone as they were dying. During the next break, while in the restroom, I felt an overwhelming sense of urgency to share my experience of Garth's death. Yet I felt an equal amount of dread at the idea of sharing with such a large group. I spoke in my mind to Padmasambhava my belief that I could not do this thing without help.

Back in the session room, the teacher continued her talk about the beneficial effects of helping someone with the dying process. With trepidation, I raised my hand.

"I would like to share an experience," I said.

"Please," said the teacher.

Knowing I couldn't turn back now, I breathed deeply and began, "My husband, Garth, died last June. He had not been a practicing Buddhist or even a meditator." I felt all the eyes on me and wondered how I could continue. Somehow I went on, explaining how I did the phowa for Garth and how he had died with that awestruck look and that half smile. When I was finished, the room fell silent. I saw in the stunned faces around me the impact of my story.

The teacher commented, "Of course, you all realize she's a plant." There was appreciative laughter. The teacher went on to suggest how my story underlined how powerful our loving help can be in the final moments of someone's life.

I sat in amazement at what had just happened. I had been able to share the single most touching and powerful moments of my life with this large group, and it seemed to be helpful. I felt something shifting inside me and I recalled how I had begged at Garth's bedside for this experience to change me into someone who could truly help others. As I walked around that afternoon, I felt a little uncomfortable with this new somewhat alien part of myself that could help others.

Later in the retreat, the teacher had us complete "one of the tasks of living and dying." In this process, we had a dialogue with someone we had unfinished business with. She also told us that someone at a previous retreat had misunderstood the directions and thought she was supposed to ask at the end of the process, "And let me hear from you." Though this had not been the instruction, this woman heard from her dialogue partner that next week.

I had desperately been wanting to hear from Garth. At the end of my dialogue with him, I wrote, "And let me hear from you."

When the teacher asked for comments about this process, I told her what I had done. She smiled, "I don't suppose you can expect a response, but why don't you continue your dialogue and ask Garth what he would say if you *were* to hear from him."

Back at home, I continued the dialogue with Garth I had begun, asking him what he would say if I could hear from him.

Annie, You need to somehow make it okay that I have died. I'm sorry this had to happen and I wish I could be there to comfort you now. Perhaps I am there somehow. You helped me so much when I was sick. You helped me more than you know as I died. It's time for you to heal and go on.

It breaks my heart to remember how you suffered, Garth. I felt so helpless. The battle kept getting more and more difficult, but I could never give up. I couldn't stand the thought of us losing. But I wish I had told you how hard it was for me to watch what was happening to you, to your body. I loved your body, sweetheart, and it was falling apart in my hands.

I hate what my illness put you through, Annie. I wish we had tried to talk. Maybe we could have been more help to each other. Perhaps we can do it now, are doing it now. Perhaps I can be with you in a way.

You know what bird I keep hearing at the house in the morning, Garth? I just heard the call now as we talk – the varied thrush. I don't remember hearing it here before, yet I've been hearing it every morning now for a couple weeks. I keep thinking somehow that you've sent them here. I know that's crazy. I love that call.

By March I was having a dialogue with Garth every morning. I had been experiencing a sense of his presence off and on, particularly in moments of intense grief when I would feel him around me. But in the dialogue, I finally felt I was hearing Garth's voice. If I hadn't been instructed to do this, I think I would have thought I really was going mad. Garth's presence was so real in these dialogues.

One morning, shortly after the Seattle retreat, I was talking to Garth in our dialogue as the tears flowed down my face. I was still in bed, but sitting up writing. A familiar call impinged itself into my consciousness from the world outside. I stopped writing and looked toward the window. The call sounded again—the single note call of a varied thrush.

I jumped out of bed, threw on some jeans, ran down the stairs, and grabbed my binoculars on my way out the door and onto the deck. I listened. The call again. I scanned the nearby cedar, wanting to be sure. Following the call I soon found the blue and orange bird with the black necklace. I didn't remember seeing or hearing the thrush here at the house before. I watched it for several minutes and heard answering single note calls from neighboring trees. There seemed to be a flock of thrushes gathered in the field in back of my house.

In the days that followed, I heard the thrush call often, most frequently in the morning, during my dialogues with Garth. I found the call immensely comforting.

One day as I walked through the Rhododendron Gardens in East Moreland, I was struck again with the void where Garth used to walk beside me. I could hardly bring myself to scan Crystal Lake for ducks, as I would normally do. I sat on a bench by the water and let the grief envelop me again. As the pain coursed through my body, I lay down on the bench. It seemed I could no longer hold my body erect. To be here in this gorgeous place without Garth was more than I could bear. How was I going to be able to stand this continual pain?

Water poured from my eyes. I felt desolate, alone. It seemed it would be a blessing to follow Garth quickly out of this sorrowful place my world had become. Dying seemed so much easier than enduring this ordeal of pain.

As I lay on the bench, drenched in my sorrow, a call penetrated my consciousness. I listened. The call came again—the single note call of a varied thrush. I felt as if it were calling to me, trying to lift me out of my blackness. I began to feel a strange comfort. It was so beautiful, this soft flute-like call. I could not remember ever seeing or hearing a varied thrush here in the gardens before. As the lone bird continued to call, I sat up and stopped crying. Then the bird fell silent.

Garth, it's raining this morning. I've heard the thrush several times while we're talking. I'm beginning to believe it is you. It would be the sort of sweet thing you would do if you could. It seems like such a clever, humorous, surprising way to respond to my request to hear from you. You always could surprise me. I loved that. I thank you for the thrush if it is you. It's such a perfect, beautiful way to let me hear from you.

When you hear the thrush call, Annie, remember that you are not alone. When you think of me, remember that I think of you. Death is not as final as we think.

I wish you were here, Garth. I wish it so badly. I wish I could see you again, talk to you.

You are talking to me, Annie. I hear you.

But if you could appear to me. It all weighs so heavy on me this morning, sweetheart. The memories of your illness, your death. I can see it all so clearly. I wish it could have been different. I wish you hadn't had to die. I know you tried. I cannot fault you for not trying.

How could I not try, Annie, when you were so determined? But we lost the battle from one perspective. There is a way in which we won. Our love grew during the most difficult time of our lives. And you helped me die well. Yes, Annie, we were also victorious.

The thrush calls, Garth. The thrush calls.

12

Janet told us she wanted everyone to do their first ritual with the class. Again, the thought of sharing with a group intimidated me, but I knew what my first ritual needed to be.

I had been using the second bedroom of my house as a depository for Garth's things, none of which I had yet been able to part with. In one corner of this room was a big pile of medical records and bills from his illness. These papers symbolized Garth's suffering to me. I sensed that by burning these papers, I could rid myself of images of his suffering that still plagued me.

I began the burning process on my deck the week before I was scheduled to do my ritual with the class. I pulled out my Weber barbecue and piled papers into it. There were papers here telling us what Garth's treatments cost and how effective they had been. I felt weighted down just by the sheer volume of this record of what we had been through. I lit the first batch and they burst into flame. Heat rose toward me. I threw on more papers, and more. The papers and the pain seemed endless.

I couldn't complete this burning in one day, but had to repeat it over several days. I saved a few of the most charged papers for my class ritual.

On the appointed night, I felt anxious, yet hopeful that this ritual would help me let go of some of my burden of pain. We were gathered in Janet's basement, where she had a fireplace. Janet had started a fire in anticipation of my ritual. I went to the front and asked for a couple volunteers to feed my papers into the fire. Two women joined me by the fireplace. I looked at the fire a moment before starting. Then I turned to the women, "As I state what I want to say goodbye to, I'll hand you a paper to put into the fire," I instructed. They nodded.

I picked up the first paper, a medical bill. "I want to say goodbye to all Garth's treatments." I handed the paper to one of my helpers. She threw it on the fire, which flared.

The next paper was some test results. I handed it to my other helper, "I also want to say goodbye to Garth's suffering and pain." The paper went on the fire.

I feared I might cry, but continued. I handed another bill to one of the women. "I say goodbye to my frustration with a medical system that couldn't help Garth." The fire engulfed the paper.

I handed the final test result to my helper. "Finally, I want to say goodbye to Garth's and my hope for his recovery." As the paper went into the fire, it flared up again. Tears welled in my eyes, but as I stared at the flames, I held them in. When I turned back to the group of about ten women, several of them were crying. I rose from my position in front of the fireplace and Janet came and put her arm around me. She said a prayer to seal my release.

I returned to my seat. I felt something had been lifted off my heart, some of the heaviness. The pain wasn't gone, but it felt diminished.

In the days and weeks after this process, I felt able to go through the room full of Garth's things. This room felt permeated with him. His hopes and dreams were filed in the filing cabinet. His past resided in the books and trunk of his treasures. His body was in the clothes and shoes. His playful spirit imbued the sports and camping gear.

Old letters from his mother touched me so much I couldn't part with them. But I began to sort through what I could let go of.

I designed other rituals for saying goodbye to aspects of my life with Garth. One of the most difficult losses for me was the loss of our physical relationship. I performed a ritual with Nancy for saying goodbye to our physical love.

I was not prepared for the impact of this ritual. Though I had been experiencing anger at my loss, this ritual unleashed my rage. Nancy encouraged me to allow this rage, and convinced me to join her group therapy where I could release it safely.

Though the rage frightened me, it also felt as if we had lanced a boil. I also tried to talk with Garth about my anger.

I'm so angry that you're gone, Garth. God, I feel this rage inside me. Goddamn it! Why'd you have to die? You just left me. You left me here alone. Why'd you leave me?!

I didn't choose to leave you, Annie. Sometimes I felt you wanted me to go. Didn't you want me to go? I got cancer, for Christ's sake, at 38! God, what a loser! I got cancer and couldn't beat it! You had to care for me. You wanted me to die, didn't you?

Sweetheart, I can't honestly say I never once wished our ordeal would end. I can't honestly say I felt no relief when you died. We had no life at that point. Our lives were all about pain. But it continues for me. My life is still about pain. At least before, we had each other. Now I'm still suffering and I'm all alone! I worry sometimes that if I had wanted your survival enough, you wouldn't have had to die. That somehow I must not have tried hard enough. But, goddamn it, Garth, you're the one who died! Why did you leave me?!

Annie, I don't think it had anything to do with you. We were fighting against something that wasn't in our control. Death is not in our control. I didn't leave you, Annie. You didn't want me gone. I died. For no apparent reason — against our will. Not by our choice. There was nothing either of us could do to stop it.

I'm sorry you had to go, Garth. I'm sorry you had to suffer so. I'm sorry if there was anything I did to increase your suffering.

I felt so inadequate. I was trying to save you. I had this flippant idea that I could save you from cancer. But what you needed was for me to be with you in a non-attached way. I was totally attached to the outcome. I would do it different now. I would focus on you more. Touch you more for you and less for me. Talk to you more for you, and less for me. Comfort you. God, I want to comfort you. It must have been so hard lying in that bed all those hours. Seeing everyone else going on. Sweetheart, I'm sorry if there was something I could have done that I didn't do.

Annie, there's always more someone could do. But what you did was enough. You loved me. What you did was a lot more than adequate. I knew you loved me. I knew you cared. A person can't ask for more than that: To have the person who loves and cares for them more than anyone — to have that person caring for them when they're dying. I was so fortunate to have that.

What happened to you, Garth, to your body, never affected my love. I felt so much compassion for you. You had to go through so much and there didn't seem to be anything I could do to stop it. I feel so much compassion, now, sweetheart, for us.

13

As June approached, it brought with it all the harsh memories of Garth's death. Janet had taught me to meet my grief with ritual, so I knew I needed to fully acknowledge this first anniversary. I planned to take Garth's ashes to Grizzly Peak, a mountain near Ashland, and scatter them. I asked Dave and Clare and Rose and her new husband Arnie to join me. Dave had just recovered from surgery to remove his prostate and was receiving chemo and radiation, but said he felt well enough to come.

We arrived on June 7 at Emigrant Lake to camp. We planned to hike up to Grizzly Peak the next day. Garth and I had spent time at the lake when we lived in Ashland, and had camped here on return visits after we left. Dave and Clare had met us here several times in the past.

As we set up our tents and prepared food, I was excruciatingly aware of Garth's absence. The light vacation tone that touched my friends' energy seemed to career off my heaviness.

Around the campfire, after we had cleaned up from dinner, I said, "In preparation for tomorrow, I want to do a ritual for saying goodbye to camping with Garth."

Though I had done several rituals, I had not yet done any with my closest friends. I felt nervous about this and worried how all this would affect Dave.

"Garth loved to camp," I started, "except when it was raining." We snickered. "We got caught in many rainstorms. I remember camping in the Marble Mountains in California one July and lying in the tent, listening to the steady rain. By morning, it had failed to let up and we decided to hike out. It is one of my fondest memories, hiking out of that steady rain behind Garth. He would still stop to look at something now and then or point something out. He was still smiling. It took us two days to dry out."

I glanced around at my friends. It looked like Dave had tears in his eyes. Clare was looking at the fire. Arnie was looking at the ground. Rose looked at me and managed a smile.

"I want to give each of you something to remind you of Garth and his love of the outdoors." I pulled out a small black mag light.

"Arnie, I give you Garth's mag light. He used this when we camped. If you have to get up during the night, may it prevent you from stumbling. May it help you see the natural world with Garth's eyes."

I handed Clare a small box. "Clare, I give you Garth's camping incense so you can bring the scent of the world he loved with you into your house. May it help you appreciate the sweet smell of the earth that Garth loved."

Next I pulled Garth's Swiss army knife out of my pack and held it in my hand a moment. It was hard to give this away—it had been such a part of Garth, present on every outdoor outing. But I wanted to give something special to Dave. I handed him the knife. "To you, Dave, I give Garth's knife that he always carried with him. It was a valuable tool on many an outdoor trip. May it serve you long and well as it did him."

Finally, I pulled out a photograph of a bull elk. "Rose," I said, "I give you this picture Garth took overlooking the ocean at Sinkyone. It was probably his favorite spot on the planet and he loved sharing it with you. May this photo remind you that you had a special place in Garth's heart."

I stared into the fire through the wetness from my eyes. I glanced at my friends: Dave was crying and the others looked near tears. We sat awhile in silence, staring at the fire, sniffling. Gradually we began to speak softly about our plans for the next day.

———

On June 8, I woke feeling surprisingly calm. After breakfast, we drove out to the trailhead in Dave's car. As we got closer we could see snow on the surrounding hills. When we pulled into the parking lot, there was snow on the ground.

"Wow, snow!" I said. "Garth would have loved this!"

As we got our packs out, Dave said to me, "You want me to carry Garth?"

I handed him the box with Garth's ashes. "We can take turns." He nodded as he put the box in his pack.

We started up the trail single file, with me leading followed by Rose, then Arnie, then Clare, and Dave. The trail zigzagged gently up toward the peak for the first couple miles. I couldn't believe the snow. It was just enough to call it snow, a couple inches, but not enough to hamper our hike. It coated our sad journey with a soft, cool beauty. About halfway up I dropped back to Dave. "Should I take Garth?"

"I've got him, Annie."

"You sure?"

"I'm sure."

When we got to the long flat top of Grizzly, I walked out to the edge that had a view over Ashland. We all stood looking out. "I think we want a more private spot," I said. "Let's keep going."

Dave and I took the lead and started checking out spots all along the top. Then we noticed that the trail went on and we joined it as it dropped down. When we had gone about another mile, a natural ledge beckoned to me. I walked over to it. A large flat rock sat like a natural altar on this spot. Parts of Ashland were visible below. I looked at Dave, "What do you think?"

"This feels right," he said.

We called to the others.

We took off our packs. Dave pulled out the box and set it down on our altar. We each had prepared a few words about what we were thankful for in our relationship to Garth, what we missed and felt we had lost, and what we regretted. When it came time to open the box, I sat and stared at it. I suddenly felt unable to do this part. The silence lengthened.

As I sat staring at the box, I felt a hand on my arm. It was Dave. "Take your time, Annie," he said. "Do you want to be touched?" I nodded. My friends' hands rested gently on my arms and legs. The tears came. I began to feel I could do this. We could do this. Together we could scatter Garth's ashes.

I opened the box. As I got up, my friends rose with me. I scattered a handful of the ashes over the ledge. We took turns dipping our hands into Garth's remains and returning them to the earth. When we were done and all in tears, Rose read a Navajo chant:

> *The mountains, I become part of it.*
> *The herbs, the fir tree, I become part of it.*
> *The morning mists, the clouds, the gathering waters,*
> *I become part of it.*
> *The wilderness, the dew drops, the pollen,*
> *I become part of it.*

That evening, as we prepared dinner, I was feeling disappointed. I had been sure there would be some sign today that Garth was with us. But there had been nothing.

The ritual had felt right. But where was Garth? We could see Grizzly in the distance and I stared up at the Peak, wondering.

"Hey," said Clare, pointing toward some nearby bushes, "What are those birds? They look like bluebirds."

Excitement immediately coursed through me and I grabbed my binoculars. Clare had grabbed hers too. I had never seen a Western Bluebird and was thrilled at the possibility of a PID. Clare and I aimed our binocs at the bushes. I caught one of the birds in my lens. It was bright blue and chestnut. Several others nearby were duller.

"We've got a little flock!" I announced.

I handed my binocs to Rose and Clare gave hers to Dave. We watched for several minutes before the birds flew off. I couldn't believe the excitement I felt simply at seeing a new bird, especially on this somber day.

Then a certainty pricked my consciousness. I said to Clare, "I wonder if that was Garth."

She looked at me questioningly.

"Garth's Aunt, who died a few years back, was a bluebird fanatic. She had houses for them all over her yard. Books about them. I wonder if those bluebirds were from Garth, his Mom, and Aunt as their way of being here to provide a little joy for us today." I felt I was stretching, maybe straining, but to my surprise Clare nodded.

"Makes sense to me," she said.

I felt a connection, almost a visitation. At the least, I couldn't wait to add Western Bluebird to my list of PIDs.

When I entered my house, upon my return to Portland, the aloneness settled around me like a dense fog. I plunged into depression.

On June 11, the anniversary of Rose and Arnie's marriage, I was on a hike in Forest Park with a friend. My somber and silent mood affected my friend and we walked along the wooded trail quietly. At one point, we stopped to sit for a few minutes. We were sitting in the sun when my friend said with surprise, "Annie, a butterfly just landed on you!" As I turned toward her, I saw a beautiful large butterfly fly from behind me and head on down the path. I was immediately flooded with the memory of what Rose had said about her wedding day a year ago—how a butterfly had landed in her hair as she talked about Garth. A small ray of awe and wonder penetrated my heaviness and I marveled at the mystery all around. Was it possible that the butterfly came again on this anniversary to remind me of eternity?

Within two weeks of our Grizzly ritual, Clare, Rose, and I all had significant dreams. Clare told me on the phone, "We were all together, Annie, with Garth, only we all know he's dying and are dealing with it. It was like we were facing this reality in a way we couldn't, when it was happening."

Rose described her dream; "I'm with Garth again while he is sick, only this time I can express my fear that he is going to die."

In my dream, Garth is at the house to greet me after my return from Ashland. His presence is so real in the dream that it feels like a visitation. As I enter the house and see him, I am thrilled and amazed. I am so happy to see him, but do not understand how he can be standing there smiling at me.

Garth takes a few things out of my hands to help me carry them up the stairs. He teases me, "You sure took a lot of things with you, Annie."

Dave suddenly comes through the sliding glass doors and is startled by Garth's presence. "Boy," he says, "a lot of people will be glad to see you!"

Garth starts up the stairs with me behind him. He turns back to me and I am suddenly overwhelmed with grief, knowing he is going to die. I drop what I'm carrying and go up to him. I hug him and say through my sudden spurt of tears, "I love you, Garth."

When I woke up, I was crying. The contact felt so real; I was with Garth and for a moment we had shared the incredible sadness of his impending death.

14

In the fall of '95, I was deep into group therapy with Nancy and decided to do her weekend workshop. Group therapy had been challenging for me from the start. I would often sit in my car outside the therapy building, trying to talk myself into going in. The words that most often succeeded in getting me inside were, "This can't be worse than losing Garth, Annie."

The central work for this weekend was to bring artifacts that represented some of our deepest pain and share their meaning with the group. I knew what artifacts to bring, but I was terrified of this process. I was still hanging back on Sunday afternoon when Nancy gave me a knowing nod. I knew what that nod meant, "Don't wait until the end!"

I got to my reluctant feet and took myself and my bag of artifacts to the front. I knew some of the people from our weekly group, but several others were new to me. We were in a semi-circle, with some folks in chairs or on couches, while others sat on the floor. I could hardly bring myself to look into the faces. I pulled a belt out of my bag and put it on the floor in front of me. Shame shivered through me.

"This belt represents the beatings my father administered to us as children," I began. "I grew to hate him for this violence." I pulled a Bible out of my bag and put it on top of the belt. "It was the Bible that told me my father was wrong. We were Christians and taught to read this book. And in this book, I found the passage, 'Fathers, provoke not your children to wrath.'"

"I remember when I first read those words that it struck me immediately as a statement about my situation. I must have been ten. From then on, I knew my father was wrong, yet I felt guilty for hating him. I used to imagine going to the kitchen in the middle of the night to get a knife. Then I would go into my father's bedroom and stand by his bed a moment watching him sleep. I imagined raising the knife up with both hands and plunging it into him."

I stopped to take a deep breath. I looked up, but I wasn't seeing clearly. I could not tell what anyone was thinking. When I pulled my next artifact out of my bag, a picture of Garth, I began to cry. Through my tears, I managed to explain, "When Garth died, my pain was so great, I thought I would die. I felt I must have been a terrible person to be punished so; that I caused this somehow, that I deserved the pain of Garth's death like I deserved my father's treatment." My tears became sobs and I couldn't go on. I looked up at the group. There was total silence. But I felt something in the room, a tenderness.

As I left the front and sat back with the group, I marveled at what had just occurred. I had shared my deepest guilt and pain with a group and they seemed to understand. And I began to see how deeply the pain of Garth's loss was imbedded in my past abuse. I felt compassion for the little girl driven to rage, the adult woman shattered by loss.

At a later training workshop to become a volunteer facilitator at the Dougy Center, learning how to help children process their grief, I was given a metaphor for my journey. In an exercise, we were asked to think of a memory, identify characteristics from the memory in our current life, and identify how we were using — or could use —those characteristics now.

The memory that floated to my consciousness during this exercise was Garth and I cross-country skiing in new snow. We had friends with us and Garth volunteered to break trail like he usually did, even though he was probably the smallest person in the group. The memory was of Garth skiing in front of our group, creating a ski track for the rest of us to follow. Being the first one to ski the track in new snow was often a tough assignment and a lot of work, yet Garth never failed in his willingness to do this for the rest of us.

In the second part of this exercise, I saw how Garth had broken trail for all of us into the realm of terminal illness and death. Since he was the first in our circle of friends, his task had been quite tough, but he made a trail that would perhaps make it easier for the rest of us.

I also saw how I was breaking trail for those around me into the realm of grief. This also was a tough assignment, but if I could lay a clear track, perhaps it would make the path easier for those who follow behind.

15

The next year, I struggled to find a direction for my new life. I continued therapy, volunteered at the Dougy Center and Hopewell House, a residential hospice, and investigated different work options. Dave continued his battle against cancer.

On Garth's birthday in March of '97, I drove out to the coast. I made a reservation at the same Inn Garth and I stayed at while we were doing the 714X treatments. I even stayed in the same room overlooking the beach. I so wanted Garth to be with me that I began to believe I was going to meet him out on the end of Cape Lookout.

I started out early from Portland and arrived in the morning with enough time to do the hike. After checking into my room, I headed to the trailhead, ignoring the steady rain. There were only a couple cars in the trailhead parking lot. The wind blew fiercely, but I was determined. I put on my rain gear and headed down the trail. The wind drove the rain into my face. I had probably only gone a quarter of a mile when I realized this was insane. The wind was like a gale that bent me over as I walked against it and the rain almost made it impossible to see where I was going. I turned back toward the parking lot with a deep feeling of loss, as if my opportunity to meet Garth had been blocked.

I got back in my car and headed to my room at the Inn. Inside again, out of the storm, I stood at the window overlooking the ocean and watched the wind and rain buffet the coast below. I had brought photo albums with pictures of Garth. While the storm railed outside, I looked through photos that told a lot of the story of my life with Garth.

In one, Garth and I stood in the front yard of our Ashland house in our wedding duds. We both looked young and happy. In another, Garth was shirtless with a day pack on. Mt. Jefferson loomed above him in the background. There was one of Garth and Rose on the floor in front of the fireplace of a past apartment, where a fire blazed. Christmas cards and stockings decorated the fireplace mantel behind and above them.

I kept going back to one photo in particular, when we were out birding, several years before he died. Garth had a full beard then and soft brown hair fell down over his forehead. I could remember the moment clearly and could see Garth standing a few feet in front of me with that bemused tolerant smile, as if to say, "Okay, Annie, you can take my picture."

I now sat in the same room he had sat in during his illness, while I had walked on the beach. All that was in this room with me now were these pictures of him. The torrential rains outside were a mere reflection of the torrent inside. All afternoon and evening I looked at photos and thought of Garth and cried for what had once been.

I had planned to head home the next morning, but when I woke and looked outside, I saw the storm had passed and left a bright sun. I realized I could probably do the hike before I headed back.

After grabbing breakfast at a nearby restaurant, I went to the trailhead. The parking lot was deserted. I would be on the Cape alone. Instead of frightening me, this fact stirred my longing again for a meeting. I figured it was more likely to happen with no one else around.

Expectantly, I started down the trail. Though walking down this path brought back many memories, the beauty helped to bring me back to the present. As the path was muddy in spots, I stepped carefully, walking on the edges of the worst mud holes. Clear sky with a few white clouds spread above. A mere breath of a breeze remained from the gale of yesterday.

With each step my conviction became stronger that Garth would be at the end of the Cape to meet me. Part of me sat in wonder at this crazy thinking. Was Annie finally going mad? it asked. But an inner knowing dwarfed this rational part. I felt certain he would be there. I even began to wonder what it would be like to see him after all this time.

Trees shroud the trail almost to the end of the Cape, but at the end the forest opens up onto a rocky finger of land jutting out into the ocean. This is where I expected Garth would meet me.

I began to pick up my pace the closer I got to the end. I couldn't wait to see Garth again. I burst through the forest onto the Cape's rocky end, fully expecting to see Garth sitting on the rocks there. The Cape appeared to be empty. I looked around, thinking perhaps he was going to come out of the woods. But there was no one.

Though the part of me that had been marveling at this insane conviction nodded its head, the part that had known he would be here could not believe it. That part was enormously disappointed. I sat down on the rocks at the edge of the Cape and stared out at the ocean. The day was gorgeous and I was at one of my favorite spots. Yet...

As I stared out to sea, I saw a very dark cloud not too far out that seemed to be headed this way. In fact, I hadn't noticed it until now, but the breeze had increased and was cooler. I decided I better head for cover back under the forest canopy and got up. The darkness was moving quickly now, my way.

I barely got into the trees before the dark cloud enveloped the Cape and began pelting tiny white hail. Suddenly, I had tiny, cold, white pellets in my hair, on my clothes, and white pellets bounced all over the ground and into the trees. I could hear the soft thuds landing in thousands of spots at once. It was so unexpected and beautiful. I was flooded with joy and a sense of Garth's presence. I stared at the miracle of white with awe and wonder.

My encounter only lasted a few minutes, but I felt its impact all the way back up the trail. When I got back to my car, the parking lot was still empty. I had been entirely alone here. Just me, the Cape, and the tiny white hail. Yet, I felt connected and satisfied now, as if I had had a special meeting.

16

In June of '97, I went for a couple weeks to Dave and Clare's to help out. Dave was still receiving treatments. He was on disability from his job as a Unitarian Minister. Though he was still mobile and independent in all his care, he looked frail and tired. He felt ill a lot of the time. During the night I would often hear him get up in the room down the hall and go into the bathroom to throw up.

During my stay, I took over the cooking and helping Dave with whatever he needed to give Clare a break. I took him to his doctor appointments and to get blood transfusions, which he seemed to need regularly. On those trips from Sonoma County to San Francisco, which took a good hour, we had a bucket on the floor next to him in case he got sick. On one of them, I asked Dave how he was doing.

"I'm just doing, Annie, doing whatever comes next."

"I have to admit, Dave, that this whole thing scares me. Are you afraid?"

Dave looked at me from the passenger's seat. "Not right now," he said, "sometimes." He was quiet a moment, then added, "Annie, you know, it's funny. I always thought I'd die from cancer like my Dad did. When Garth died, he showed me that it was possible. He showed me that I could do it too, if I had to."

I studied the road ahead. "Do you think that is where this is headed?" I asked.

"I don't know, Annie. I really don't. There's a bell curve of possibilities. On one end is a cure; on the other is death. I'm hanging onto both ends of that curve, trying to believe and hope for total remission, while at the same time allowing the possibility of my death from this."

The road before us had blurred and I raised a hand to wipe my eyes. "I love you, Dave," I said. "I don't want you to die."

"I know Annie."

"Do you think your Zen is helping you with this?"

"Having practiced for ten years probably helps me sit with what is, Annie. I don't know."

We got to the hospital and I parked. We were here for a transfusion, because Dave's platelet count was low. When he was all hooked up, with the life-giving fluid dripping into him, we sat next to each other reading magazines.

———

In 1978, Dave and I had been married 8 years. We had experimented with an "open marriage" a few years earlier to try and unravel Dave's disturbing attraction to other women and our sexual difficulties. After a couple years of relationship mayhem, where we both took lovers outside our marital bond, we had decided to renew our vows and monogamy.

We had been seeing a new couple, Harriet and Frank, who were becoming friends. Harriet, an artist, had asked me to pose for a portrait. I had agreed and began spending hours in her studio just sitting. She told me she liked my high cheekbones and angular chin.

One day, Dave came to me while I prepared dinner in the kitchen of our house in Fairfax, California. "Annie," he said, "Can we talk?"

I looked up at him from my chopping task. His hair was reddish gold and his chin shaved clean. He had a curly red moustache. He looked much the same as he had looked back in 1967 when I had first spotted him in the opposite stands of a gymnasium at a Letterman concert. He was with a woman my brother had dated and my eyes kept going back to him throughout the concert. Something about that fluffy bright hair offset by the deep red moustache attracted me. I wouldn't actually meet him until 1968.

"Annie," Dave started. "I want to preface this with the understanding that you have total say in this. I will not do anything you don't want."

I studied Dave's face, trying to corral my thoughts. What now? Where was this going? There was urgency in Dave's tone.

"What is it, Dave?" I asked.

"It's about Harriet and I, Annie," he said earnestly. "We've become attracted to one another."

I immediately felt irate and betrayed. "You've talked about this?"

"Yes," he admitted, "We would like your permission to act on our feelings. It is okay with Frank."

I couldn't believe this. Not again. And I couldn't believe the betrayal from Harriet. I was allowing her to paint my portrait!

"The three of you have talked about this?" I asked, incredulous.

"Not exactly," Dave backed off. "Harriet talked to Frank."

I didn't say anything for a moment as I tried to remain calm. How could Dave suggest we go through this again? I knew it was not an option for me anymore and I knew I could never see Harriet again.

"Dave," I said, as calmly as I could. "I cannot do that again. If you are giving me the option to say no to this, that is my answer."

Dave grimaced, but seemed resigned. "That is your answer?"

"No question."

He never mentioned it again. He knew at this point that his choice was to stay with me and corral this thing, or give it free reign to drive us apart forever.

17

I went to spend time again with Dave and Clare during Christmas of '97. I had just begun a Master's Program in Social Work the previous fall. Rose picked me up at the airport and took me to where Dave was in the hospital because he'd had seizures. We walked into the hospital room just as a couple orderlies wheeled Dave into the room on a gurney. Clare walked alongside. "Hey guys!" she greeted us cheerily.

Dave raised his head slightly from the bed and looked at me. He held out a hand in my direction. "Annie," he said.

I took his hand and squeezed. I tried not to cry at the change in him. His golden hair was gone and there was no curly red beard. His face looked swollen. He smiled at me with such sweetness, I thought my heart would break.

When they got him into the bed, Rose, Clare, and I took seats. "Hey," Dave said, "My three favorite women!" We all laughed.

A dark-haired female doctor came in shortly to give us the results of Dave's tests. She was blunt and to the point. "The cancer has gone to your brain," she told Dave. "Your platelet count is 38,000. You could bleed to death at any moment." She didn't stay to pick up the pieces of her shattering announcement.

We all sat stunned. Dave began to cry first. Clare and Rose and I went to him, sitting close on the bed, holding his hands and touching him. We were all crying.

Dave spoke first, "I guess this is it."

We looked at him.

"There's nothing left for us to try."

"We wish there was," said Rose.

Dave nodded. "But there isn't." He looked at each of us and then said to Clare, "So, we have to let go." He paused. "I want to go home." He looked at me. "Can we get me home?"

Rose stayed with Dave while Clare and I went to make the arrangements. We needed huge oxygen tanks delivered to the house, because Dave could hardly breathe. We arranged an ambulance to take him.

At home, we set up shifts for staying with Dave through the night. Mine was the first. Dave was lying on a hospital bed in the living room with his head propped up. The oxygen helped him breathe.

I was helping him drink some water, when he looked at me. "Annie," he said. I felt the word all the way down to my toes. He dozed most of my shift. When I rose to go, he opened his eyes, "Give me a kiss," he asked.

I kissed him lightly on the lips.

"Again," he asked.

I kissed him again.

As I headed away from the bed, he lifted an arm to wave. I waved back.

Around two a.m., Rose came into the bedroom where I slept. "Annie, he's going."

I jumped up and followed her into the living room. Clare stood next to Dave's bed, where he lay unconscious, breathing that labored, and intermittent type breath I knew too well. I tried to do the phowa for him, but felt resistant and unprepared.

We three stood by his bed as he breathed his last. When he was still, Clare jumped up to start making arrangements, as certain things had to be done to prepare for the three day vigil planned according to Dave's Buddhist tradition.

Rose and I stayed by the bed. After a few minutes, Rose turned to me, "I feel joy, Annie! I feel happy!"

I did not understand her feeling, but I believed it was somehow from Dave. Perhaps the end of the bell curve he found himself stuck with was not so bad after all.

———

It was 1969, the summer of love. In August, the "All you need is love" counter culture movement culminated with Woodstock, where rock greats like Janis Joplin and Jimi Hendrix performed. Crosby, Stills and Nash's hit single "Suite Judy Blue Eyes" blared on the radio.

"Butch Cassidy and the Sundance Kid" lived and died at the cinema.

Dave and I went on a trip that August with friends, camping in the only woods we could find near Chicago. We had known each other just about a year. I attended university west of Chicago and Dave drove out most weekends on his motorcycle to see me.

We were camping this hot August weekend in our friends' camper. I already had two dozen mosquito bites driving me crazy. Dave and I headed out alone one morning on a hike. "There's something I want to show you, Annie."

As we trudged through tall grass, my mosquito bites itched and I worried about ticks. I had no idea where we were going or what Dave wanted to show me. I only hoped it was worth my discomfort.

"There it is," said Dave. He pointed to an old shack about a football field away.

I felt slightly annoyed, wondering about being dragged out to this shack, but I didn't say anything.

When we got to the shack, Dave led me around to the other side and up onto the porch there. We stood on the porch looking out at nothing but miles and miles of corn in the distant fields. "I've brought you here for a reason," said Dave.

I looked up at him. He turned and went to a corner of the porch. From that corner he picked up what seemed to be a brand new broom that had apparently been leaning against the abandoned old cabin's wall.

"Annie," said Dave. "I would like to give you this engagement broom. It represents our willingness to set up house together and to work together to keep that house clean." He paused, looking at me earnestly. "Will you marry me?"

He had caught me totally by surprise. We had not talked of getting married. But how could I refuse an engagement broom? When I said yes, he handed me the broom. Though marriage had not been in my mind, it felt natural, Dave's hand in mine.

18

In the summer of '98, Clare and I arrived first at Emigrant Lake. We had our eyes on the same campsite we'd been in three years ago, but someone was camped there. It looked like they were about ready to break camp, so we perched at a nearby site like vultures, waiting.

Over an hour later, Clare turned from our conversation while we sat on a picnic table to evaluate the movement at our coveted site. "Sure looks like they'll be out of there soon," she said.

"Taking their sweet time," I commented.

A ranger's truck pulled up to our site and a middle-aged guy in uniform got out. "You ladies planning on staying the night?"

"We're waiting for friends and to see if those folks vacate that spot," Clare indicated our quarry.

"You like that spot?"

"Well, we're kind of attached. We've stayed there before," explained Clare.

The ranger pointed down the hill. "You might check out number ten. It's vacant and I think it's the best in the place. Big enough for several tents too."

"Want to check it out, Clare?" I asked.

Clare shrugged and nodded.

We thanked the ranger and walked down the hill. It was a warm July day and we both wore shorts and t-shirts. We walked into number ten. Immediately, a bird flew onto a branch in the tree above us.

"Hey," said Clare. "A bluebird!"

"Wow!" I said.

We watched it a moment in the tree and then it flew into a hole in the tree right at the center of the site. Soon another bluebird joined it in the hole. Clare and I looked at one another. "They're nesting here, Annie!" she said.

"I guess this is our site," I replied.

We didn't even need to discuss it. When Rose and Arnie arrived, we were set up in number ten. We showed them the nesting bluebirds.

Every time I saw the bluebirds, I had a strong sense of Dave. It would be just like him to not mess around, to make sure we saw the bluebirds, to have them *nesting* in our site.

The next day, we hiked the trek up to Grizzly Peak, taking turns hauling Dave's ashes. There was no snow. The day was clear and warm, with a bright sun. I could almost see Dave with us. He would have a hat on, long sleeves and pants, and sunglasses to protect himself from the sun. He would blow his nose a lot. The Dave I pictured still had that red blond coloring. He would have punctuated our journey with the occasional joke.

Clare had brought a picture of where we had scattered Garth's ashes off a ledge so we could find the same spot. When we found the natural ledge, we took off our packs. Clare set up a little Buddha and Dave's Zen bowl to use for a gong, and tried to light a candle. But a slight breeze foiled these attempts. Arnie constructed a little candle sanctuary out of stones and we finally got our candle going. After a Zen chant, we meditated for a few minutes.

Rose and I had known Dave for 30 years. We had both met him in '68 at summer school in Wheaton, Illinois. Dave told me later that after meeting us, he decided to take out "one of the twins." He ran into me first after this decision, which was lucky for us both; I don't believe Rose would have gone out with him.

Clare had been married to Dave for more than 13 years. Only Arnie had not known Dave well.

When we moved to the ledge to scatter Dave's ashes, I could not believe he was not with us. Dave had become such a permanent part of my life. I knew him when he was young and confused, when he went from teaching to working for the post office to nursing. It wasn't until he met Clare that he found his calling as a Unitarian Minister.

He had been my husband, the man I thought was the "one." He had become my closest lifelong friend. And now he was dead, gone.

After scattering Dave's ashes, we sat silent a few minutes watching the candle on the ledge burn. The memory of Dave's final kiss floated to me. He was so sick then, yet his essential sweetness shone through. Dave had grown from that confused young man into someone who could embrace his own death with grace. I felt privileged to have known him.

We began to tell our favorite memories of Dave. Clare held up a picture that she felt captured her favorite feeling of him. In the picture, Dave is standing on a down log in an old growth forest. He is dressed in white pants and shirt, wearing a broad-brimmed white hat. His stance is like a dance step, his feet apart on the log, his arms spread like he's at the end of some performance. Dave's red-bearded face stares out at the camera with an expression of sheer delight.

"This is how I remember you, Dave," said Clare.

Rose's favorite memory was at the hospital when Dave recited to her part of his favorite poem by Rainer Maria Rilke, "The Man Watching":

> *I can tell by the way the trees beat, after*
> *so many dull days, on my worried windowpanes,*
> *that a storm is coming,*
> *and I hear the far-off fields say things*
> *I can't bear without a friend,*
> *I can't love without a sister.*

All I said was, "I will always remember, dear Dave, that you were the one who came when Garth died."

In the summer of '68, I was looking at potential textbooks in the bookstore at the summer school Rose and I were attending. Rose had decided to attend nursing school the next fall and I was planning to go to University. This would be our last summer together. We had chosen to room apart for the first time to provide somewhat of a gradual transition to our new separate lives in the fall.

The man with long reddish-blond hair and a full, curly red beard, whom I'd met a couple days ago, walked into the bookstore. As soon as he saw me, he came over.

"You're one of the twins," he said.

I couldn't deny it. "Guilty," I said.

"Are you Annie or Rose?"

"Annie," I admitted.

"Would you like to go for a motorcycle ride, Annie?" he asked.

I was young and just beginning to fledge. A motorcycle ride sounded scary enough to be appealing. "Okay," I offered. "Your name is Dave?"

He smiled and nodded. "How about tomorrow afternoon?"

We made the date.

The next afternoon, when he came to pick me up on his bike, I felt excited and scared. I was going on a motorcycle ride with a guy who looked like a hippie. I knew my parents would not approve.

Dave's bike was a small one. I got on behind him and he told me I'd better hug him to stay on. We sped off. We rode on streets for a few minutes until he pulled into some woods. I wondered what this was about. He said, "Hang on!" as we dropped down onto a dirt trail. His bike ground and skidded through the trees. We headed down into another dip and he lost control for a moment. We toppled over.

As we picked ourselves up, Dave said, "I'm so sorry! Are you alright?"

I nodded, but my nervousness must have showed.

"Don't worry," he said. "That won't happen again."

We got back on the bike and Dave drove carefully out of the woods into a clearing. He pulled up to an area with a series of cages and shut off the bike.

"This is a little preserve I wanted to show you," he said.

We walked up to the first cage, which enclosed a barn owl peering out at us from its perch on top of a ledge.

"This is a wildlife preserve," explained Dave. "They take birds and animals injured somehow and try to rehabilitate them."

I looked around. "This is really cool," I said. Dave talked to one of the birds and I stole a look at him, wondering. I felt drawn to him.

After a bit, he turned to me, "Well, Annie, ready to take your life into your hands and get on that bike with me again?"

"Okay," I said.

And off we went.

19

By the summer of '99, I had graduated with a Master's in Social work. I worked as an on-call hospice social worker while I looked for more permanent work. I felt thrust into my new role prematurely, despite my training. I felt unsure about this new life I had chosen. I still missed Garth and still grieved Dave. I decided to escape to the woods for a few days.

I drove up to Mount Hood and set up camp at McNeil. No one else was in the campground. For some reason this did not alarm me, but rather gave me hope that I would receive the guidance I sought. I hoped for contact with Garth and Dave somehow, thinking this would give me the reassurance I was looking for.

Though the day had been warm, the night was cool as I sat huddled by my lone campfire. I had started the fire early for warmth and the sun had not yet set. I heard the distinctive sound of a nighthawk as it swooped down over my fire. Following it back up, I saw its white barred wings.

Immediately I thought of that summer with Dave and Clare, when they saw and heard their first nighthawks. Soon nighthawks were swooping and soaring all over the sky. Their presence brought me some comfort and I no longer felt alone.

I had planned to hike to Ramona Falls the next day, but I woke the next morning with a paralyzing depression. It was all I could do to struggle out of my tent and make coffee. I managed to get a fire going and sat staring at the flames with my mug. I couldn't even put words to the darkness enveloping me. I could barely move. I went back to the tent and lay on my bag for hours, frozen in hopelessness. I found it hard to imagine getting up ever again, let alone going out in the world to do social work. What had I been thinking? Who did I think I was to be able to help people? How was I to go on so alone?

I managed to get up again about noon and make another cup of coffee. I stirred the fire, added wood, and got it going again. I tried to think about food. I thought perhaps I could manage a simple sandwich, but could only eat half of what I made. I wrapped up the rest and put it back in the ice chest.

I contemplated a walk, but my legs felt like lead. I went back into the tent. As I lay on my bag staring out through the tent opening at the forest I was in, I felt an incredible sadness. I felt entirely alone. This place held memories of the great togetherness I had had, but it was gone now. Never again would Garth or Dave be here with me. Never again.

I might be alone for the rest of my life. I certainly would never see either of them again. What did I have to look forward to? What did I have to hope for? More suffering and pain? Even if I met someone, one of us would eventually leave the other alone again. Even if I met no one, I'd have to face Rose's death, or she would have to face mine.

I remembered asking Dave at one point, during my final days with him, "Tell me Dave, what do you think is the point?"

He had looked at me and said, "I'm surprised you would ask that, Annie." He sat in the only chair he was comfortable in by then, his face swollen from the drugs, his hair mostly gone. But he smiled at me as he said, "The point is just to be, Annie. That is all."

The tears joined this memory in my tent in the forest. I still did not understand the point. And I wished Dave could be here to explain it to me. Where were those guys and why were they gone? What was to become of me? What should I do with this remaining life? I cried and cried until sleep rescued me.

When I woke, I saw the light was fading. I dragged myself out again and got the fire going. I forced myself to finish the sandwich. When the nighthawks started, I sat by the fire staring up at them. The darkness in the outer world was beginning to mirror the one filling my mind. Yet, these birds, these amazing creatures of the evening, seemed like glowing embers of hope in my ashy darkness.

The next morning, both the interior and exterior darkness had lifted. I got up and marveled at the glorious day. Part of me kept rummaging through the cupboards of my mind, looking for remnants of yesterday's gloom. This peace and happiness that now graced my morning felt a little suspect.

I fixed breakfast and packed a lunch for the hike to the falls. Yesterday almost seemed like just a bad dream. I felt anticipation about the hike and hope for some kind of sign from Garth and Dave. It all seemed possible this morning. I felt buoyed by the solitude with only the natural world as my companion.

I headed down the Ramona Falls trail about ten a.m. I took the high side of the loop first, that afforded views of Mount Hood. I had only been on this loop for about a half mile, when I thought I heard a nighthawk. I looked up and there it was swooping in the sky above me. Then I saw another and another. I got out my binocs and watched while a small flock of nighthawks entertained me with their aerial displays for about five minutes. Then they were gone. I wondered about their daylight presence and kept thinking of Dave's thrill at seeing them.

I went on toward the falls, feeling that Dave had made himself known, but there had been nothing from Garth. I did not think I should expect anything after all this time, but I wanted a reassurance that I was not alone.

I took off my long-sleeved shirt as the day and the hike grew warm. Vistas of Hood appeared at spots along the trail still showing a lot of snow for so late in summer. The earth on this part of the hike was dry, whereas the lower loop, after the falls, followed a creek through the forest. This trail sported rock croppings and huge boulders, contrasting the lush green below.

I heard the water's roar and knew I was close. I put my shirt back on in preparation for the sudden drop in temperature that I knew was coming. When I entered Ramona Falls space, I felt awe at the sheer volume of water tumbling down in a massive sheet. Though I had seen it many times, I was always amazed. I looked around and saw that I was alone here. I had expected something or someone? Garth? Dave?

I found a spot to sit and pulled my lunch out of my pack. I sat eating and watching the water. I felt a heaviness, yet I was calm. Of course there was no one. There had been no cars at the trailhead. But I wasn't looking for someone with car keys in their pocket.

I almost chuckled to myself at my own insane inner conversation. Was I crazy? Or just lonely?

As I mulled this over and watched the falls, a gray jay flew into the space between me and the falls. Another jay was chasing it and landed in the tree directly in front of me. Wait a minute...

Suddenly, I was flushed with excitement as this bird cocked its head at me. I grabbed my binocs and aimed them at my avian visitor. I had known before my binocs brought it into focus, but still I felt a tingling sensation like I had been touched, when my magnified eyes confirmed that it was a varied thrush peering at me from the tree's limb.

"We shall not cease from exploration

And the end of all our exploring

Will be to arrive where we started

And know the place for the first time." (T.S. Eliot)